HISTORIC SITES & LANDMARKS OF NEW SMYRNA BEACH

HISTORIC SITES & LANDMARKS OF NEW SMYRNA BEACH

ROBERT REDD

THE History PRESS

Published by The History Press
Charleston, SC
www.historypress.net

First published 2015

Manufactured in the United States

ISBN 978.1.62619.766.4

Library of Congress Control Number: 2015949882

Contents

Acknowledgements

New Smyrna Beach is a city with almost 250 years of history. Not many locations can say such, and it is certainly something to promote and be proud of. Despite this long history, the city has often been ignored in favor of longer-established St. Augustine and Pensacola or more glitzy cities such as Orlando and Miami. There is a lot of great history here and many wonderful stories. Along the way I have met many tremendous storytellers.

I first want to thank the Southeast Volusia Historical Society for allowing me to serve as executive director at the New Smyrna Museum of History. This is truly a dream job, and I enjoy going to work every day. Not many people can honestly say that, and I know I am lucky.

There are so many talented volunteers at the museum that it would be impossible to thank them all. Some deserve an individual mention, however. Irene Beckham has been overly generous with her research, her knowledge and her time. She got me started working on the correction of several sacred cows in the city, such as the story that New Smyrna added Beach to its name when the city merged with Coronado Beach. She has provided excellent source material about the Pacetti Cemetery in Ponce Inlet, the early years of the historical society and other areas. Without her research, which she so freely shared, much of this book would not be here. She is truly a gem, and I am proud to call her a friend.

Dave Miner is research librarian at the museum, and he helped locate many items that were needed. He and retired librarian Joan Westhrin spent many hours filing and cataloguing books, photos and documents. Their work, while not complete, made my trips upstairs much easier.

Zelia V. Sweett has generously searched through her family photographs and allowed me to use several of them. They have greatly improved the visual part of this book, and I am extremely grateful to her for her contribution.

Barbara Zafuto has done much research on Hannah Bonnet, the first female mayor of New Smyrna Beach. She portrays Hannah during the cooler months of the year and offers walking tours that cover historic aspects of our city. Several little nuggets from her have made it into the book, and I thank her for sharing her knowledge. If you are in the city during the months of January through April, I highly suggest taking one—or all—of her tours. They're not just educational but also entertaining.

Some of the first people I met at the museum when volunteering were Lynn and Drew Mays. They have been nothing but wonderful and encouraging to me, and I thank them both. To the dozens of other volunteers who have not been named, I send my thanks for your support and encouragement. You make our museum the gem that it is!

Jimmy Harrell at the Mary S. Harrell Black Heritage Museum helped fill in gaps about the history of St. Rita's and also Glencoe-Geiger Cemetery. It's just a shame so much black history has been lost in our community.

Johnny Bledsoe, the city clerk for New Smyrna Beach, along with Dave and Barbara, helped put together the listing of New Smyrna Beach mayors. There are still some gaps in the early years of the city, but this list is a tremendous help and giant step in the right direction.

Andrew Foster has supplied much information on his ancestors, the Coe family, who helped found the Glencoe area of New Smyrna Beach. He has freely provided copies of documents and newspapers to our museum, and for that we are extremely grateful. He has also generously provided photos that I was able to choose from for this book.

These wonderful people and others, who have given me so much, have made this book what it is. For any errors, however, I must take responsibility.

To my friends Jim Schmidt, Michael C. Hardy and Dr. Nick Wynne, thanks for the encouragement and positive words. I've heard it from every one of you that with each book you write you find several more that need to be written. Those words are 100 percent correct!

Thanks to everybody at The History Press for your continued support and for backing me on my second book. Here's to a long relationship!

My parents, Ted and Bonnie, have shown through their actions the importance of loyalty and dedication. I learned a solid work ethic from them, and I keep trying to "do good work." Thanks for your support. I love you.

Last but certainly not least I must thank my wife, Christina. She has supported my work on this the entire time and has offered numerous suggestions that have been incorporated here. She has gone on multiple outings to take photographs and has patiently listened as I have tried to work out what should go where in the text. Many have been the nights when she has fed three hyperactive large dogs so that I could finish "just this last little bit." The dogs and I both thank and love her.

Introduction

The city of New Smyrna Beach is one that can trace its roots back almost 250 years as of this writing. This is an incredible achievement and serves to place the city as the third oldest in the state of Florida, behind only St. Augustine and Pensacola. While there are those who would argue New Smyrna (now Beach) is actually older than either of the two prior mentioned cities, there is no credible evidence to back that claim. Personally, I am happy to say New Smyrna Beach is the third oldest.

While the city is almost 250 years old, that does not mean it has been largely populated for the entire time. Many of these years, there were only a handful of inhabitants. The 1900 United States census showed only about 1,200 residents. By 1940, there were approximately 5,100 residents, and currently there are nearly 24,000 permanent residents calling New Smyrna Beach home. This number swells by several thousand each winter as northerners flock south looking to enjoy the balmy climate.

The history of New Smyrna Beach, however, is one that is not well documented. Certainly, we know about Dr. Andrew Turnbull and his attempt to establish a settlement here. What we don't have is much in the way of tangible documentation. The archaeological evidence is fairly slim, with much of it no doubt buried under modern roads and homes. This makes it doubly important that when an opportunity comes along to dig on a piece of property in the known settlement area, it be taken advantage of. We have letters written by Turnbull and his associates, but we don't have letters to and from the Minorcans and others who lived here.

More modern history becomes problematic as well. There were several county histories written during the early years of the twentieth century. These had little to say about New Smyrna, however. In more recent years, there have been a couple of books that have helped outline some of our local history. None of these has attempted to tell the "story" of New Smyrna Beach. For current and future writers, this has proven and will prove to be quite the dilemma. Where to begin? What are the main sources and are they readily available? Which oral history stories should be believed and how do you begin to corroborate them?

As I began thinking about this project, I decided to try to avoid some of these issues for the time being. Instead of writing a town history, I would put together a book outlining historical spots and areas of the city. I would then try to tell the story of these places. Why is a sugar mill located on Old Mission Road? What's the story behind that modern-looking monument in Riverside Park? Why does city hall have a piece of modern sculpture in front? These are the types of questions we are asked at the New Smyrna Museum of History. Why not give locals and tourists the story behind these places.

I have attempted to cover the major historical locations in and around New Smyrna Beach. Did I get them all? No, of course I didn't. The limits of time and space mandated that I stop at some point. For instance, the history of the railroad in New Smyrna Beach is one that should be told. I have not told it here, however. It really did not fit in with my goals and ideas for this book. For those looking for a broader look at the Florida East Coast Railway, there are several good books available. In addition, much of the rail history would be inaccessible to visitors. This is a book for locations you can safely and legally get to. You really don't want to deal with a railroad "bull."

I have also downplayed Turnbull-era sites such as the canals. Why, you might ask. To adequately cover the importance of the Turnbull settlement in the history of New Smyrna Beach would take an entire book of its own. There are scholars such as Dr. Roger Grange, Dot Moore and Dr. Dan Schafer who are making tremendous contributions toward our understanding of colonial-era New Smyrna.

My hope is that this book is not just read but also used. Get out of your chair and go take a look at some of these locations. There is great history in New Smyrna Beach. Sometimes, though, you just need to know where it is hidden!

1

Spanish Mission or Sugar Mill

It is never too late to rectify a mistake or an untruth.
—Charles H. Coe

There are several locations in the New Smyrna Beach area that have sparked controversy over time. The large coquina ruins located just off Highway 44 is one of those areas. Today, there is little doubt about what the ruins are, but that has not always been the case. There are two main characters in the story of the ruins: Jeanette Thurber Connor and Charles H. Coe.

Mrs. Connor was the second wife of the wealthy Washington Everett Connor. The Connors, who married on May 1, 1913, were separated in age by twenty-three years. Mrs. Connor passed away at age fifty-five after a lengthy illness. Washington Connor outlived his younger bride by almost eight years and passed away at age eighty-six. Despite her young age, Mrs. Connor developed a reputation for her research into early Spanish settlements in Florida. She gathered a large amount of documents from sources in Spain. She and John B. Stetson co-founded the Florida State Historical Society (not to be confused with the Florida Historical Society that is still in existence). It was through the FSHS that she published several volumes of translations. Much of her research material now resides in the Library of Congress. Today, however, she is known for the controversy surrounding the coquina ruins in New Smyrna Beach, and her reputation has been diminished due to her incorrect views and conclusions.[1]

The other major player in regards to the history of the ruins is "Captain" Charles H. Coe. Coe was a man who dabbled in many things and accomplished much in his life. Coe was born in 1856 in Connecticut and died in 1954 in Florida. During his lifetime, wars from the Civil War through the Korean conflict were fought. The majority of his life was spent in the newspaper and writing industry. By age twelve, he had his first newspaper job at the *Appleton Times*. By age twenty-one, in 1877, he had begun the *Florida Star*, and by 1890 he had launched the *Highlands Star*. Perhaps he is most remembered for his book *Red Patriots: The Story of the Seminoles*. Samuel Proctor said about Coe in the introduction to the Bicentennial Florida Facsimile Series version of the book:

> *By describing the life of the Seminoles, Coe made a considerable contribution to Florida history since so little was known of their life style in the post–Civil War period. Like Helen Hunt Jackson in* A Century of Dishonor, *Mr. Coe attempted to prick the conscience of the nation in* Red Patriots. *He wanted the people of Florida to redeem their honor by recognizing the legal and property rights of the Seminoles.*[2]

Captain Charles H. Coe, seen here in a 1943 photo, stands aboard the *Buccaneer II* in West Palm Beach, Florida. Coe was a newspaperman and writer, and his family helped found the town of Glencoe on the western side of New Smyrna Beach. His work is instrumental in clarifying the history of the local sugar mill. *Courtesy of Andrew Foster, great-grandson of Charles Coe.*

We are most interested in Mr. Coe, however, for his short booklet *Debunking the So-Called Spanish Mission near New Smyrna Beach*, which he published in 1941 near the end of his life. Here, Coe outlines his reasons for stating that the ruins are those of a sugar mill that was destroyed by Seminole Indians during the Second Seminole War.[3]

A large arch that is a part of the sugar mill ruins is among the reasons Jeanette Connor and others thought the ruins to be of religious origin. For many years, the story was told that these ruins were a Spanish mission, with some thinking their origin went back to Christopher Columbus. *Courtesy of the author.*

Historian Gary Luther said it well when he claimed, "Northern newspapers have always had a flair for the fantastic when relating events in the South." Luther was directly referring to a March 4, 1894 issue of the *New York Herald*. The *Herald* ran an article that day titled "May Be America's Oldest Building: Picturesque Ruins of a Venerable and Mysterious Structure in South Florida. WAS IT ERECTED BY COLUMBUS?" With more than a century of scholarship at our fingers, we know this claim to be ludicrous; however, in the pre-Internet days, the romantic language used by the *Herald* could easily sway less informed readers about the age and original use of the building. This article makes several wide leaps of faith that have no basis in the historical record. Phrases such as "it is but reasonable to presume"; "allowing for the imperfect state which the art of navigation had at that time reached"; "if this landing was made, what more natural than that at New Smyrna"; and others would give any modern critical reader pause.

A lengthy quote from the Reverend J.A. Ball is used to help further the image that the ruins are those of some religious group:

> *There may be a difference of opinion as to the use for which this building was designed, and the time when it was built; but here we have the form of an ecclesiastical edifice of the Spanish style of construction, just such a building as we would expect an old mission house to be. We have the Oriental court common in Eastern countries and in Spain, and the cross has such measurements as give due proportion to the structure, showing an effort of architectural skill and a purpose that it should not be taken for anything but a religious emblem.*[4]

Early county histories written by men like T.E. Fitzgerald and Pleasant Daniel Gold only helped perpetuate the story of the ruins being of religious significance. Fitzgerald goes so far as to rehash the theory of John Y. Detwiler that New Smyrna Beach is older than St. Augustine. Fitzgerald says of the local ruins:

> *The Old Spanish Mission immediately West of New Smyrna Beach is evidence of early Spanish occupancy, and whether the location was the original St. Augustine will always be a matter of dispute, especially when the circumstantial evidence of records of latitude found in old Spanish documents are taken with some allowances, considering the crudeness of mariners' instruments of the Sixteenth Century, in identifying the localities of today.*[5]

The story of the Connor involvement in the ruins begins in 1893, when Washington E. Connor paid Isadora Matthews $400 for a ten-acre plot west of town proper that contained the ruins of an old building. Isadora was the widow of William Lourcey. By 1870, she had married Emanuel J. Matthews. Captain Matthews received a seventy-seven-acre land grant from the United States government in 1878 that contained the ruins. He would pass away in 1890, and the twice-widowed Isadora sold part of the property to Connor.

Emanuel Matthews would accidentally play a role in promoting the view that the grounds were religious in nature rather than industrial. In 1881, Matthews was tilling ground near the ruins in order to plant turnips. It was while doing this that he unearthed the remains of three bronze candlesticks. In 1925, the earlier mentioned John Y. Detwiler made a trip to Spain, carrying large and detailed photos of the candlesticks. Detwiler searched many cathedrals for a match to the square-based objects with no success. His final conclusion was that

> *the parts of three Bronze Candlesticks, found in the Old Mission near New Smyrna, have been proved to be of Moorish origin, having square bases, emblematic of the materialist elements of earth, air, fire and water—words which would indicate an antiquity even greater than the discovery of America,*

> *or the conquest of Moorish possessions by Spain…in repairing the cathedral in Seville shortly after the Moorish conquest, every effort was made to eradicate the materialistic emblems embodied in the square, typifying earth, air, fire water. In the case of the candlesticks it was only necessary to loosen the rod, remove the base, supply it with another of triangular form and the work was done.*[6]

While Detwiler was claiming the sticks to be older than the known European discovery of the continent, others were claiming them to be of American colonial origin.

As mentioned previously, Washington Connor married the much younger Jeanette Thurber in 1913. For Jeanette's birthday in 1914, he gifted to her the parcel containing the ruins west of New Smyrna. Mr. Connor knew his new bride to be a budding historian and that this would be a gift she would treasure. Mrs. Connor's scholarship later included a biography of Pedro Menéndez de Avilés and the first two of a proposed ten-volume collection of *Colonial Records of Florida* that was to cover the Spanish occupation from 1570 until 1700.

Through her extensive research, Mrs. Connor believed that sometime around 1693–95, a group of Franciscan monks requested assistance from the Spanish crown in order to build three missions south of St. Augustine that would minister to the needs of the local Indians. The crown responded by sending a large assortment of tools, including two hundred large hoes, six large saws, six small saws, fifty machetes, four large augers, four medium-sized augers and four gimlets—tools that were used by the monks and Indians to build the three missions: St. Josef, Tissimi and Atocuimi. Atocuimi was the name of the mission Mrs. Connor claimed was located at New Smyrna.

The Indian tribe that was said to be in the New Smyrna area was the Jororo (pronounced Ho-ro-ro). The Jororo first receive mention in Spanish documents in 1690. The tribe lived in the area south of the Matanzas River, in modern-day St. Johns and Flagler Counties, and in between the St. Johns River and the Atlantic Ocean.

In 1727, an epidemic of unknown variety eradicated the Jororo population. According to Mrs. Connor, the ruins then sat unused until the arrival of Dr. Andrew Turnbull and his indentured servants, who were the first to use the building as a sugar mill. The machinery now found at the mill was not brought by Turnbull but is of a later time, according to Connor. In fact, it is now believed the grinders and kettles were brought by Thomas Stamps sometime around 1825.[7]

It is agreed that the building on the property was destroyed in a late December 1835 attack at the start of the Second Seminole War. After that event, the land and building were unused.

This view shows several of the arched windows that led some to believe the ruins were those of a Spanish mission. In fact, the ruins date to around 1830, when William Depeyster and Eliza and Henry Cruger had a sugar mill built. The mill was destroyed on Christmas Day 1835, during the Second Seminole War. *Courtesy of the author.*

Mrs. Connor used her influence to have a large historical marker placed on the property in 1925. The marker, whose story has since been successfully challenged, now resides in the collection of the New Smyrna Museum of History. The marker reads:

This Mission
Built for the Jororo Indians
By Spanish Franciscan friars
about the year 1696, is
preserved as a memorial of
the forty-four missions of
Spanish Florida
To commemorate
the service and heroism
of the Franciscan fathers
in the ancient Florida missions
this tablet is placed here by
The Florida State Historical Society

The Florida Daughters of the American Revolution
Washington Everett Connor
Jeannette Thurber Connor
1925

The Florida State Historical Society referenced on the marker should not be confused with the Florida Historical Society that today is based out of Cocoa. The society associated with Mrs. Connor was started by her in partnership with John B. Stetson Jr., the future United States minister to Poland, a position he held from 1926 until 1931.

In the fall of 1926, Mrs. Connor fell sick and for many months was confined to the home of her mother in New York City. She passed away on June 9, 1927, and was laid to rest in Green-Wood Cemetery in Brooklyn. She did not live long enough to complete her volumes of Spanish records translation, but she also did not live long enough to see her theories about the mysterious ruins in New Smyrna debunked.[8]

This is a detailed view of the plaque that used to stand at what are now acknowledged to be the ruins of an early nineteenth-century sugar mill. The theory that these ruins were a Spanish mission has been thoroughly disproven. The original plaque is now on display at the New Smyrna Museum of History. *Courtesy of the author.*

In 1941, Charles H. Coe set out to put on paper his ideas about the origins of the ruins so long thought to be a mission. In fact, Coe uses a very pointed pencil to show where he feels he was correct and the Connors were wrong. Coe makes convincing arguments, but readers must first acknowledge his error in attributing the mission theory. Coe gives credit to Washington Connor, rather than Jeanette Connor, for putting forth the mission theory. Perhaps a minor error considering the overall time period—an era when women

Postcards such as this helped spread and perpetuate the myth that these ruins were those of a Spanish mission. This card estimates the origins of the ruins to date to 1696 rather than the correct date of 1830. *Courtesy of the author.*

were still usually at home and few married women worked outside the home. Still, it is an error that must be acknowledged.

Coe outlines nine reasons that he claims help prove that the ruins could not be those of a mission but rather were of later construction (i.e. a sugar mill). Coe's first claim deals with the hostility of the Indian population in the area. He outlines several instances of violence directed at white settlers. Coe summarizes, "But the reader already knows that the white man could not have existed on this site in the year 1696."[9]

Coe's second reason is that he sees no purpose for an expensive mission to be built in this location considering the Castillo de San Marcos had been completed just a few years earlier and the Matanzas Inlet, a pathway to St. Augustine, did not have a proper fort. The third argument Coe makes deals with the appearance of the masonry. Coe points out that it all appears to be of "identical character and material in general." To him, this proves the building was not adapted from a mission to a later use as a mill. If that were the case, there would be differences in the materials. Here he also makes the claim that there is no similarity in design between the ruins and buildings of Spanish design.[10]

Coe returns to his youth in order to put forth his fourth argument. He remembers visiting the ruins for the first time in 1874. He remembers the coquina ruins being "quite fresh and clean" and not having a moss accumulation as might be expected from an older building. Coe also points out the rooms in a building plan and that each corresponds to a particular use in a mill. "There was no indication of, nor room, for 'friars' cells' 'chapel' 'refectory' 'dining room' or 'confession windows.'"[11]

The fifth through eighth reasons are closely related and shall be dealt with together. The ruins at New Smyrna are compared to those of the known Bulow mill, located to the north in Flagler County. To Coe, these buildings are almost identical. While the area had a low population, Coe could find no settlers who recalled having heard that it was ever anything but a mill. These witnesses included perhaps one of New Smyrna's most famous settlers, Jane Sheldon. Coe even uses this to attack the theory that Andrew Turnbull had turned the ruins into a mill. He emphatically stated about Turnbull: "Did not use the building and that it was not even there at that period." Coe's seventh piece of evidence is that he could find no writings from prior visitors to the town mentioning the ruins. He also asks why the Catholic Church did not make a claim of some kind and notes that priests from St. Augustine were quiet about this "mission." The eighth reason Coe uses to attack the mission theory takes us to the state of Georgia. In Georgia, several sets of ruins were said to have been missions only later to have those claims disproven. If that were the case in Georgia, it would stand to reason the same could be said in Florida.[12]

Coe's final attack on the Connor theory settles on an 1835 U.S. survey of the area that lists the property as being a sugar mill. No mention is made by surveyor F.L. Ming that the property and building had ever been anything other than a sugar mill. Captain Coe uses this final chapter as a plea to have the offending plaque with the Jororo legend removed from the property.

Coe's arguments were persuasive enough that T.E. Fitzgerald, the former mission promoter, wrote in the introduction to the pamphlet, "The reading of Captain Coe's manuscript has convinced me that he is right in his conclusions—as I believe it will convince any reasonable person who has made a study of historical facts and fictions relating to Florida."

Charles Coe was not one to back away from a fight, and he knew this pamphlet would create controversy. He ends his work saying, "The writer is well aware that he who shatters an idol is more or less unpopular. But the surgeon's knife is used that good may follow, therefore, 'Let justice be done though the heaven's fall.'"[13]

What we do know about the ruins has been confirmed through the archaeological work performed by John W. Griffin from the Florida Board of Parks and Historical Monuments. Griffin found no Spanish artifacts and also that the "chapel" area matched the machinery room at the Bulow Plantation. He stated the ruins were from the early 1800s and were those of a sugar mill.

Looking through one of the large archways, a visitor can see three large kettles that were used during the drying process. By using these vats, both sugar crystals and molasses were recovered. Molasses was a key ingredient in making rum. *Courtesy of the author.*

Sometime shortly before 1830, William Depeyster, along with Eliza and Henry Cruger, purchased land from Ambrose Hull. In 1830, William Kimble began construction on a sugar mill for Depeyster and Cruger. The soon-completed mill was put to immediate use. Cane from the surrounding area was brought to the mill, where it was rolled through the iron presses. The juice that was extracted would then be put into cooking kettles and turned into syrup. The syrup was then cooled in large storage vats. After cooling, sugar crystals became separated, and molasses could be drained off. Molasses was highly prized and was used to manufacture rum.[14]

Despite the overwhelming amount of evidence supporting the ruins being a sugar mill, there are still those who are not fully convinced. Harris Samuels wrote a brief piece for the Southeast Volusia Historical Society newsletter that shows he was not fully convinced regarding the accepted view of the sugar mill. He ends by saying, "It is inevitable that in a community so rich in history as ours that there be some controversy. It is also premature to conclude that this debate is over."[15]

Let us also not forget that the sugar mill ruins are located just off Old Mission Road!

2
Cemeteries

Don't die old, die empty. That's the goal of life.
Go to the cemetery and disappoint the graveyard.
—Myles Munroe

With a history approximately 250 years old, it would seem that New Smyrna Beach would have several old and possibly large cemeteries. This is not the case, however. There is only a small handful of cemeteries associated with New Smyrna Beach. Two are small church-related grounds, one is a city-owned lot that is no longer open for burials, one is a historically black cemetery and the last is what could be called the "historic" cemetery and is still open for burials. Farther to the south in Edgewater is a modern cemetery that is often used by residents. This cemetery, Sea Pines, will not be discussed. At this time, archaeologists have discovered no burial locations for the Turnbull settlement. Should a Turnbull-era cemetery be discovered, it would be a major archaeological find.

Detwiler Park Cemetery

This small, inactive cemetery, which used to be called Coronado Cemetery, is located beachside on Oakwood Avenue adjacent to a children's playground and some tennis courts that were built in 1972. The grounds are now

John Detwiler was one of the early settlers of Coronado Beach. He bought beachside property during an era when it was not fashionable. Detwiler was a believer that New Smyrna was settled earlier than St. Augustine and put together a pamphlet outlining his argument. His daughter, Florence Hannah Detwiler Bonnet, would become the first female mayor of New Smyrna Beach in addition to being a successful realtor. *Courtesy of the author.*

owned by the City of New Smyrna Beach. The roots of the cemetery go back to 1904, when John and Ella Detwiler deeded a two-acre property to Herbert Longstreet, Arthur Miller, William Newell and Claude and John Vrooman with two conditions: first, a cemetery association was to be formed that would sell lots at a reasonable price or provide them free of charge should a family not be able to pay, and second, a town hall was to be built for what was then Coronado Beach. The first burial was that of Roderick

Douglass, who passed away in 1906 at the age of fifty-two. His wife, Edith, who was twenty years his junior, was buried beside him in 1960.

By 1953, with Coronado Beach and New Smyrna having become one city, there was no need for a town hall. The Coronado Cemetery and Improvement Association deeded the property to the city with the same stipulations it had received with the property.

The cemetery property seems to have been little used. In total, there are fewer than seventy-five headstones showing. By the 1970s, burials had pretty well come to a halt, with only six stones showing dates from that decade. The most recently dated stone is from 1984 and belongs to Una Capps Douglass, who passed away just short of her ninety-third birthday.

As for the Dewiler family, John and his wife are not buried in the cemetery. His daughter, Florence Detwiler Bonnet, and grandson James Andrew Goodwin are buried there, however.[16]

EDGEWATER–NEW SMYRNA CEMETERY

While not actually located in New Smyrna Beach, Edgewater–New Smyrna Cemetery is the cemetery that people think of when talk of a historic cemetery comes up. Located on U.S. 1, this cemetery is approximately thirty-five acres and contains over ten thousand interments. In recent years, the cemetery has added an area devoted to veterans and also has added more niches based on the increase in the number of cremations.

The cemetery has burials that are dated to the 1840s and 1850s, well before the cemetery was in existence. These remains were originally buried elsewhere—many believed to have been interred in what is now downtown New Smyrna Beach on Faulkner Street.

An early pioneer of the area, John Milton Hawks donated land to the City of Hawks Park for a library, city hall and cemetery. Up until 1910, Hawks kept a handwritten journal detailing burials and other important information. When he passed away that year, the journal disappeared for several years before turning up in some of his papers.

A walk through Edgewater–New Smyrna Cemetery is like a walk through the history of southeast Volusia County. Perhaps the most important burial here is that of Dr. John Milton Hawks (1826–1910). Dr. Hawks was a surgeon, businessman, abolitionist, author and founder of Hawks Park, now known as Edgewater.

He received his medical degree in 1847 and during the Civil War served as assistant surgeon to the Thirty-third United States Colored Troops (USCT) before being appointed surgeon for the Twenty-first USCT. In 1865, he helped found the Florida Land and Lumber Company and established Port Orange. This business helped provide jobs and homes for former slaves, many of whom stayed in an area of Port Orange known as Freemanville in the years after the business failed. In 1871, Hawks established Hawks Park, the city that was to become Edgewater in 1924. Hawks passed away in 1910. His wife, Esther, a doctor and educator in her own right, passed away in 1906 and is buried at Pine Grove Cemetery in Manchester, New Hampshire.

Ernest William Gautier served as a Democratic state senator from 1951 through 1966, representing the twenty-eighth district, which included New Smyrna Beach. Gautier was instrumental in firming up the finances of Edgewater–New Smyrna Cemetery. His plan created a trust fund with part of the proceeds from lot sales that was to be used by the cemetery only. This allowed for long-term care and maintenance of the cemetery. *Courtesy of the State Archives of Florida.*

One of New Smyrna's earliest families, the Murrays, may be best represented by Jane Murray Sheldon (1812–1903). In 1835, Jane married John Dwight Sheldon, and they moved to New Smyrna. It was here that they built a hotel on top of the midden and coquina foundation in Old Fort Park. This hotel was said to be about sixty rooms and the grandest south of St. Augustine at the time. In 1864, the hotel was shelled by the Union ships *Oleander* and *Beauregard*. Already a widow, Jane bravely rebuilt, but on a much smaller scale. This building served as a boardinghouse, general store, print shop and port collector's office. The structure lasted until around 1903, when it was demolished. Jane Sheldon passed away in 1903. Research shows early burials such as Mrs. Sheldon's were done on land located near Faulkner Street in New Smyrna Beach. They were later moved south to the more formal Edgewater–New Smyrna Cemetery, where they were reinterred, many with new headstones.

Fraternal organizations are well represented in the cemetery, and Caspian Hale, a leading member of the Elks, is a prime example. While it is often misrepresented that Hale himself founded the Elks (the Elks were founded in 1868, and Hale was not born until 1888), he was a leader in the state organization. He served as exalted ruler and district deputy grand exalted ruler and was president of the Florida State Elks Association.

State politicians are represented by state senator Ernest William Gautier and James Updegrath Gillespie. Gautier was a conservative Democratic state senator who served in Tallahassee from 1951 to 1966. It was through his efforts that the Edgewater–New Smyrna Cemetery finances were put in order. A portion of each plot's sale is now reserved for cemetery use, including maintenance and perpetual care. Gillespie served in the state legislature and was a chairman of the Utilities Commission. According to a pamphlet published by the cemetery, he was an expert on Greek and Roman coinage and was the author of several books on the subject.[17]

A modern Confederate military headstone marks the grave of William Rowlinski, Company A, Thirty-fourth South Carolina Infantry. Rowlinski, a native of Russia, served as the first principal keeper of the Mosquito Inlet (now Ponce Inlet) Lighthouse. He served there from 1887 until 1893. *Courtesy of the author.*

It must be remembered that Florida was a part of the Confederacy, and several Confederate soldiers are buried here. These men, some of whom were civic leaders in the early days of the community, include Benjamin Fox, C.B. Futch, Thomas G. Marlow, Henry Joseph Michael, William Robinson, William Rowlinski (the first principal keeper of the

Mosquito Inlet Lighthouse), Rhodolphus Swift Sheldon (this is the spelling on his headstone, but his name is often found spelled Rudolphus) and Frank Sams. While the local Sons of Confederate Veterans has compiled this listing, there does not appear to be a similar listing for Union soldiers.[18]

GLENCOE-GEIGER CEMETERY

The historically African American Glencoe-Geiger Cemetery is located north of Highway 44 on Sugar Mill Drive. In recent times, a bike path and associated parking lot have been built on land adjacent to the cemetery. Despite what some might call an intrusion, the cemetery has retained its charm, and volunteer workers keep up with maintenance of the property.

The cemetery can trace its roots back to the 1880s, when it was originally a small cemetery for the white Smith family. There are five headstones related to the Smith family: A.C., Mary, Nancy, Edward and a baby. The Smith family

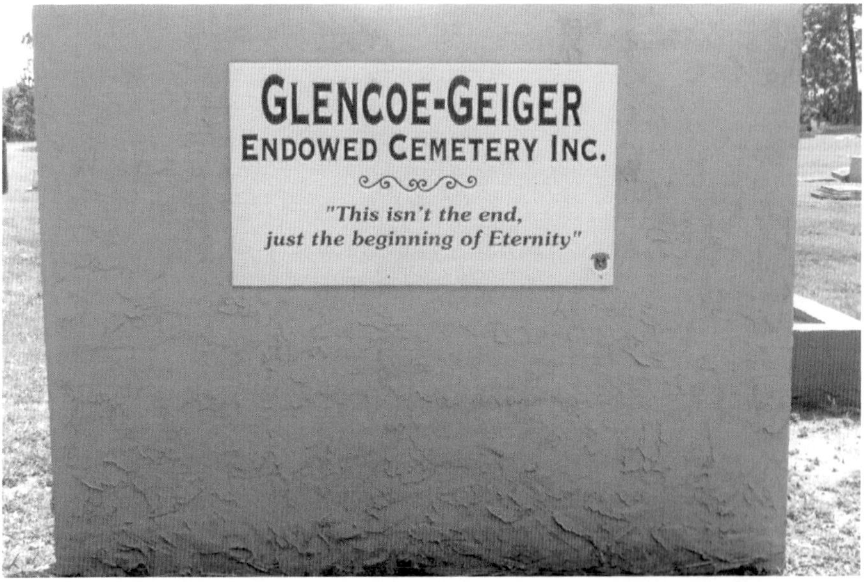

Glencoe-Geiger Endowed Cemetery is a traditionally African American burial ground. Despite many earlier burials, the current management structure of the cemetery was formed in 1949. Buried here are Henry Rhodes, the first African American city commissioner in New Smyrna Beach, and humanitarian Lydia Pettis, creator of the Forgotten Christmas Tree program. *Courtesy of the author.*

Tradition says that only one white family is buried in Glencoe-Geiger Cemetery: the Smith family. Archibald Curry Smith served in Company B, Fifth Florida Cavalry, during the Civil War. The Smith family, who owned the property, are said to have deeded the property to the Geiger family for use as an African American cemetery. *Courtesy of the author.*

member who may be most remembered is Archibald Curry Smith. A.C., as his headstone reads, lived from 1826 until 1892. What makes Smith stick out so much is that he served as a captain in the Fifth Florida Cavalry, Company B, during the Civil War. He enlisted in 1863 and was paroled in 1865. The Fifth Florida spent the majority of its time in north Florida engaging in minor skirmishes. It did, however, have a role during the Battle of Olustee and also during the Battle of Natural Bridge. The battalion surrendered in May 1865 at Tallahassee. A Confederate burial in a black cemetery is certainly not an everyday occurrence.[19]

According to the USGenWeb, the Smith family deeded the property to the Geiger family for use as an African American cemetery. This same listing, however, shows no known Geiger burials there. It could be that the family did not have lasting headstones. In addition, many records and burials have been lost to time.

In 1949, the Glencoe-Geiger Endowed Cemetery Corporation was formed to manage the cemetery. Unfortunately, it appears that for many years the cemetery was overlooked. Due to that, and its remote location, the cemetery grounds became the target of vandalism, theft and illegal

Glencoe-Geiger Cemetery is home to monuments of all kinds. In the foreground, note the homemade headstone lovingly created for Irene Jackson. In the background are markers as diverse as funeral home metal signs, professionally carved headstones and government-issued military headstones. Heritage is important here, and culturally indicative signs—such as shells on burials—are commonly seen. *Courtesy of the author.*

dumping. In 1987, a chapel was added to the property. In more recent years, a dedicated group of volunteers has been working to bring the property back to life. Work has been done to restore the chapel; vandalism has been fixed where possible, though some headstones show evidence of having been used for target practice; and the four-acre property has been cleaned up. With a new bike and walking trail located near the cemetery, there is more traffic through the area, and hopefully that will discourage the illegal activities that have plagued the grounds in the past.[20]

Bethel Baptist Church is now in charge of making burial arrangements. Currently, there are approximately nine hundred marked burials and an unknown number lost to the ages. Prominent burials in the cemetery include humanitarian Lydia Pettis and Henry Rhodes, the first black city commissioner in New Smyrna Beach.

3
Downtown New Smyrna Beach

So go downtown,
Things will be great when you're downtown,
No finer place for sure, downtown,
Everything's waiting for you.
—*"Downtown," composed by Tony Hatch and sung by Petula Clark*

Canal Street is the major road in downtown New Smyrna Beach. It runs from off Highway 44 on the west side of the railroad tracks all the way to the Indian River. If somebody tells you she is going "downtown" in New Smyrna Beach, it's a solid bet she means Canal Street. Here you will find restaurants, shops, the Utilities Commission building and more.

Sams Avenue is located in downtown New Smyrna Beach and runs north of Canal Street. Sams Avenue is the second road west from the Intracoastal Waterway. Currently, the corners of Sams and Canal are home to a restaurant and parking for the Southeast Volusia Chamber of Commerce Building. Many of the areas that follow are located on Sams Avenue.

The name Sams is synonymous with the history of New Smyrna. Frank W. Sams (1846–1921) was an early settler of the area, Civil War veteran, hotel owner, politician and noted hunting guide. A walk through the local Edgewater–New Smyrna Cemetery turns up more than a dozen members of the Sams family.[21]

NEW SMYRNA MUSEUM OF HISTORY

This postcard view of the New Smyrna Beach Post Office shows the beautiful five-arched building that today houses the New Smyrna Museum of History. The building was constructed in 1925 and was designed by Edward Wilson. The post office stayed in this building until 1967, when it moved to Canal Street. *Courtesy of the author.*

The five-arched, two-story building located at 120 Sams Avenue that is now the home to the New Smyrna Museum of History has not always housed a museum. The building was originally a post office; it served as home to the Utilities Commission and now houses the museum.

A plaque on the building indicates that the land was the site of the first school building in New Smyrna and in all of Volusia County. The school was built in 1872 at a cost of forty-two dollars. Frank W. Sams, the owner of the Ocean House, which at the time was located directly in front of this property facing the Indian River, employed Delia Stowe as a nanny. Ms. Stowe was to become the first teacher at the new school. By 1901, the local school was located on Mary Avenue; it was used by students until Faulkner Elementary opened in 1916.[22]

The beautiful five-arched building, now home to the New Smyrna Museum of History, was originally built as a post office. In early 1925, the U.S. Postal Service accepted a bid from Edward Wilson, who was to construct a new building for the growing town and lease it to the United States government. The annual lease amount was for $2,400, compared to the prior location's leasing cost of $1,500. The new facility provided more room for the growing service. The postal service remained on Sams Avenue until 1967, when it moved into a newer and larger building at the corner of Rush and Canal Streets. Postal operations would remain in the downtown area until 1989, when a new and modernized facility was opened on Mission Road.

As a point of interest, builder Edward Wilson had a peculiar way of marking his buildings so that people could identify them. On the front of the building, along the top edge, he would have a "W" put into the facing. This inconspicuous mark can be seen in several buildings located in the downtown area today. Mr. Wilson is buried in the Edgewater–New Smyrna Cemetery located on U.S. 1.[23]

In 1968, the city acquired the building from Mr. Julius J. Yambor for $60,000. For a short while, the Parks and Recreation Department operated some of its programs there. In 1975, the Utilities Commission left city hall and put its administrative offices in the building. As New Smyrna Beach continued to grow, so did the Utilities Commission, and in 1998, the UC, as it is commonly known, moved to its current home, the Southeast Bank building on the corner of Magnolia and Canal Streets.

During the 1920s, Edward Wilson and his brother, Francis, were real estate developers and builders. Wilson is credited with building the local post office, a structure that has since housed the Utilities Commission and now the New Smyrna Museum of History. His builder's mark, a large W, can be seen near the roofline of this building. *Courtesy of Zelia V. Sweett.*

The story of the museum is also the story of the Southeast Volusia Historical Society. With a long history in the area, there was a strong need for such a society, but until Ray Goodrich and Marvin Age met with Mayor George Musson and Harold Cardwell to discuss the idea in June 1982, there was no organized group promoting, researching and preserving the area's history. A public meeting to gauge interest in the project was held on June 30, 1982, in the DeBerry Room, located in what was then the Southeast Bank building (now the Utilities Commission building).

More than fifty people attended the organizational meeting to learn why an organization of this type was important. At the end of the meeting, fifteen of those in attendance agreed to take part in an organizing committee. On July 2, this meeting was held in the office of local attorney Clay Henderson. During the meeting, the first executive members of the board of directors were chosen: president, Marvin Age; first vice-president, Larry Sweett; second vice-president, Ray Goodrich; recording secretary, Dot Moore; corresponding secretary, Sandy Sweat; treasurer, Dorothy Miller; and curator, Harold Cardwell. Regular board members elected were Harold Cardwell, Priscilla Cardwell, Dot Moore, John Bornman, Lucille Bornman, Lois McFadden, Dorothy Miller, Wallace Spears, Madalon Reichold, Leila Wilsey, Sally Gillespie and Ray Goodrich. The first official meeting of the Southeast Volusia Historical Society was called to order on July 29, 1982, in the DeBerry Room of the Southeast Bank.

Lawrence J. Sweett was a driving force in the early days of the Southeast Volusia Historical Society. He was a three-time president of the board of directors for the society. In addition, he served as a New Smyrna Beach city commissioner and was also a member of several city and county boards. He was the son of local historian Zelia W. Sweett and an author in his own right. *Courtesy of Zelia V. Sweett.*

During the early years of its existence, the historical society displayed artifacts wherever possible: at city hall, the chamber of commerce and wherever else secure display space could be found. When the Connor Library building move was complete (discussed in much further detail elsewhere in this chapter), a seemingly permanent home for the society and budding museum had been found. It would not be long though before a larger location was needed.

The old post office building was a natural fit—a historic building for the historical society. Two problems immediately came up. First, the building was in a terrible state of repair and needed a large amount of work. Second, the building was only being leased, and the city retained ownership. When the society applied for a Special Category grant from the State of Florida Division of Historical Resources in order to make needed repairs, it was denied because it did not own the property. The City of New Smyrna Beach again showed its generosity and deeded the property to the historical society, allowing it to reapply to the state and this time be awarded more than a quarter of a million dollars for repairs and renovations.

With funding now available, work began in earnest, and by the end of January 2003, the New Smyrna Museum of History had opened its doors to the public. Many of the first exhibits worked hand in hand as fundraisers for operating costs. As part of the original displays, ninety-three photos from the Zelia Wilson Sweett collection were enlarged and sponsored by the public at a cost of $100 each. These sponsorships raised almost $10,000 in seed money for operating costs. At the time, there was also a large model railroad display that showcased what the Florida East Coast Railway looked like during its heyday in the city. The "train display" proved very popular with younger visitors and is still remembered today.

Those who lived in Central Florida during the summer of 2004 cannot help but remember the multitude of hurricanes that hit the state: Charley, Frances, Ivan and Jeanne. Unfortunately, the museum building would become a victim of Hurricane Frances in early September. As winds higher than seventy miles per hour barreled through the area along with huge downpours, New Smyrna Beach found itself without power, and many areas were flooded. The beachside was completely evacuated, and residents were not allowed to return home. The museum suffered major roof damage along the front of the building, the portion facing east, which received the most direct hit. Fortunately, the interior damage was contained, and there was limited display damage. The museum was closed for more than four months, however, to fix the roof and walls and make other needed repairs. A

New Smyrna Beach used to be a major hub of railroad activity. Strikes by Florida East Coast Railway employees led to massive changes in the industry in the region and ended local passenger rail. This early 1960s photo shows the train station and signage for the Railway Express Agency. Changes in how freight was shipped in the post–World War II era led to the closing of the business. During its early years, the New Smyrna Museum of History was home to a popular model railroad based on the real rail yard in town. *Courtesy of the author.*

silver lining came out of the damage, though. Upon removing the destroyed carpeting and multiple layers of floor covering, beautiful hardwood floors were discovered. This original feature of the building is now one of the first features a visitor notices upon walking in the front door.

In May 2004, when the coming tragedy of hurricanes was not a thought in anybody's mind, the society submitted another grant request to the state, this time in an attempt to design and create a new display that would be dedicated to the Turnbull settlement. This grant included a significant amount of back-up documentation, including results of multiple state-funded archaeological survey projects that found Turnbull-associated items. What perhaps put the historical society over the top in this request, though, was a discovery of information in Dundee, Scotland.

In 2002, historical society president Dave Borland fielded a call that ultimately led to a gentleman by the name of Colin MacIntosh. Mr. MacIntosh was a volunteer at the Dundee City Archives and, during his work, had discovered three maps in the collection of Sir William Duncan, physician to King George III. Duncan was a partner of Dr. Andrew Turnbull in setting up a settlement in Florida with the main goal of being an indigo plantation. This plantation would be started by using indentured servants, mostly brought from the Mediterranean area of Europe. The majority of laborers were Minorcan, Greek and Italian, though there were other nationalities as well. There were also enslaved Africans among the workers.

What Mr. MacIntosh found proved to be invaluable. In addition to letters sent by Turnbull to Duncan, there were detailed maps showing the settlement's outline. These maps showed the settlers' houses lined up for over seven miles along the Hillsborough (now Indian) River, adjacent to agricultural fields. Near the wharf area, the maps show a cluster of more than thirty buildings. Information like this has proved to be of vital importance for emergency archaeological work should a more modern property be demolished or should a property owner wish to disturb the soil.

With this information included in the grant proposal, there could be little doubt of the importance of the Smyrnea settlement, and in June 2005, the historical society was awarded $250,000 for the design and creation of what came to be "the New Smyrna Settlement" display, along with a corresponding display around the outside perimeter of the museum known as "the Timeline."

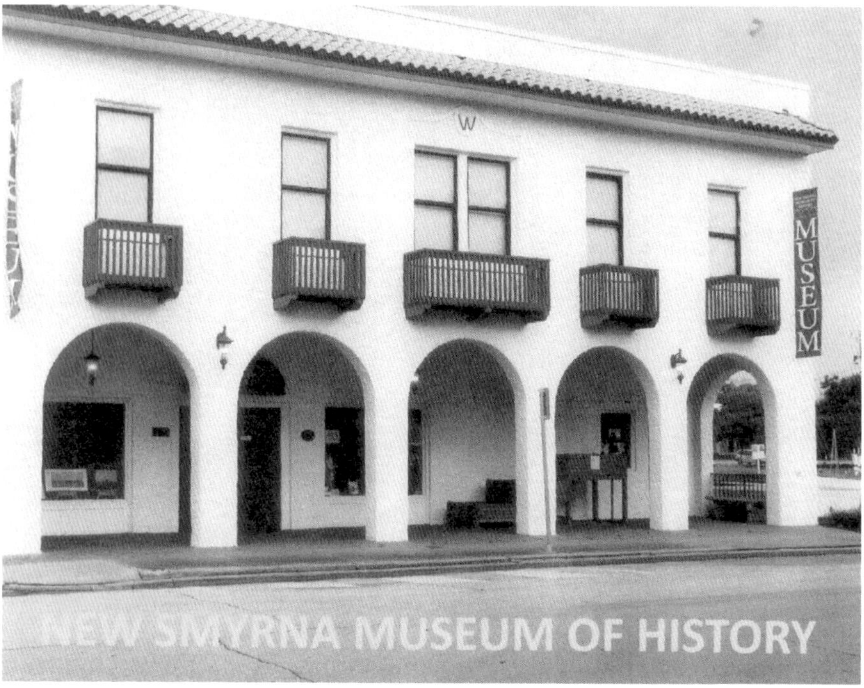

Originally built as a post office, the building constructed by Edward Wilson—note the "W" near the roofline—is now home to the New Smyrna Museum of History. This award-winning museum is home to the Zelia Wilson Sweett collection of artifacts and much more dealing with the southeast Volusia County area. *Courtesy of the author.*

With the decision made to include a major Turnbull settlement display, the railroad display was displaced and the owners removed it. The professionally designed and built Turnbull settlement display opened in November 2006, right on schedule. In 2007, the historical society was awarded a Florida Preservation Award for Meritorious Achievement in the Field of

Zelia Wilson Sweett was a noted authority on the history of the southeast Volusia County area. She had a particular interest in Native Americans and developed a large collection of artifacts, many of which are now housed in the New Smyrna Museum of History. Mrs. Sweett was the founder of the Jane Sheldon Chapter of the Daughters of the American Revolution. *Courtesy of Zelia V. Sweett.*

Education/Media for the Turnbull Colony Exhibit from the Florida Trust for Historic Preservation. It was also awarded a Florida Preservation Award for Outstanding Achievement in the Field of Education/Media for the film *Smyrnea: Lost and Found.*

The Turnbull display features several short videos, an interactive computer exhibit, artifacts and more. The exterior timeline begins with ancient fossils and works through the major timelines in Florida history, all with focused emphasis on events that happened in the area of southeast Volusia County. The Zelia Wilson Sweett photos still hold a place of honor in the display and are complemented by artifacts and relics that have been donated to the museum.

The museum is rounded out with the North Exhibit Room, which is used for short-term exhibits usually put together by local organizations. Examples of exhibits that have been shown include NASA, the Civil War, the sixtieth anniversary of the cease-fire agreement in Korea, the citrus industry and many more. Upstairs at the museum features the Zelia Wilson Sweett collection of relics and artifacts. This wonderful collection includes arrowheads, pottery and other Native American pieces. Also upstairs is the Sheldon Research Library, which houses books, photos and other research items dealing with the southeast Volusia area. The library is open by appointment.

In recent years, the museum and historical society have grown so much that a paid employee was needed, and in October 2012, the first paid executive director, Leigh Finner, was hired on a part-time basis. She began the work of moving the museum forward before resigning to accept an out-of-state job. In March 2014, a second executive director, Robert Redd, was hired. The addition of this position has relieved the board president of the day-to-day management activities and also provided a "face" to the community.

The museum has become an important part of the New Smyrna Beach community. Events such as monthly Community Museum Meetings, book readings and more take place on a regular basis. In 2015, the museum was host to a traveling exhibit sponsored by the Smithsonian Institution. "The Way We Worked" proved a huge success, and visitors during the six-week exhibit more than doubled from the previous year. The future is indeed looking bright for the New Smyrna Museum of History.[24]

EMORY BENNETT PARK

Located directly across the street from the New Smyrna Museum of History sits a small park with a flagpole and a coquina monument dedicated to Emory Laurence Bennett. Bennett was born in New Smyrna Beach and grew up to the south, in Cocoa.

While Bennett did not live a long life—he lived only twenty-one years—he is remembered throughout Central Florida for what he did. Bennett is

Private First Class Emory L. Bennett (December 20, 1929–June 24, 1951). Bennett is the only individual born in Volusia County, Florida, to have been awarded the Medal of Honor. Bennett was killed during the Korean War while helping to protect fellow soldiers. He has monuments, roads and hospitals named in his honor. *Courtesy of the Southeast Volusia Historical Society.*

currently the only person from Volusia County to have been awarded the Medal of Honor. Private Bennett was posthumously awarded the medal for his actions during the Korean War.

Emory Bennett was born in New Smyrna on December 20, 1929. In 1936, the Bennett family moved south to Cocoa, where he finished high school. He then moved to Jacksonville and began attending Jones Business School. Bennett enlisted in the army on August 25, 1950, and by 1951, he was on active duty in Korea. He served as a private first class in B Company, Fifteenth Regiment, Third Infantry Division.[25]

Bennett's actions on June 24, 1951, are best summed up in his Medal of Honor citation, presented in December 1951:

> *Private First Class Emory L. Bennett, Company B, 15th Infantry Regiment, 3d Infantry Division, distinguished himself by conspicuous gallantry and intrepidity at the risk of his own life above and beyond the call of duty in action against an armed enemy of the United Nations, near Sobangsan, Korea, on June 24, 1951.*
>
> *At approximately 0200 hours, two enemy battalions swarmed up the ridge line in a ferocious banzai charge in an attempt to dislodge Private Bennett's company from its defensive position. Meeting the challenge, the gallant defenders delivered destructive retaliation, but the enemy pressed the assault with fanatical determination and the integrity of the perimeter was imperiled.*
>
> *Fully aware of the odds against him, Private Bennett unhesitatingly left his foxhole, moved through the withering fire, stood within full view of the enemy, and, employing his automatic rifle, poured crippling fire into the ranks of the onrushing assailants, inflicting numerous casualties.*
>
> *Although wounded, Private Bennett gallantly maintained his one-man defense and the attack was momentarily halted.*
>
> *During the lull in battle, the company regrouped for counterattack, but the numerically superior foe soon infiltrated into the position.*
>
> *Upon orders to move back, Private Bennett voluntarily remained to provide covering fire for the withdrawing elements, and, defying the enemy, continued to sweep the charging foe with devastating fire until mortally wounded.*
>
> *His willing self-sacrifice and intrepid actions saved the position from being overrun and enabled the company to effect an orderly with-drawl. Private Bennett's unflinching courage and consummate devotion to duty reflects lasting glory on himself and the military service.*[26]

In the years that have followed, Emory Bennett has received numerous recognitions from his boyhood homes. On October 10, 1963, the Emory Bennett Causeway, a thirteen-and-a-half-mile stretch of State Road 520 between Cocoa and Port Canaveral, was dedicated. In 1993, the Emory L. Bennett Memorial Veteran's Nursing Home was opened in Daytona Beach. A bronze sculpture created by artist Tom White was unveiled in Riverside Park in Cocoa in February 2007.

Bennett's hometown of New Smyrna (now New Smyrna Beach) honored him in November 1994 with a ceremony and monument dedication. A large group—including Bennett family members, veterans (including some who served with Bennett), U.S. representative John Mica, Mayor George Musson and the general public—paid their respects to Private Bennett and others who have served their country. The ceremony included a color guard out of Fort Stewart, Georgia, and a fly-over by four F16 fighter jets stationed at Homestead Air Force Base. By the end of the service, more than a dozen groups had placed floral wreaths around the beautiful monument that serves as a reminder that any person, no matter where they are from, can become a hero.[27]

CITY HALL AREA

The city hall building itself did not start out life as such. In the depths of the Great Depression, the Work Projects Administration, as the WPA was called after 1939, helped create work for millions of unemployed men building roads, public buildings and more. New Smyrna Beach was the recipient of some of this government spending. The building that now serves as city hall was constructed through the WPA at the then staggering cost of almost $125,000.

During the March 17, 1941 dedication ceremony for the new Cultural Center building, Dr. Max Bernd-Cohen commented on why he thought the building was constructed: "We have faith in ourselves and as men and women living in a democracy and are conscious of ourselves as human beings [and] because the people who will enter the center in future years will be enriching their lives for future generations." He finished with the observation: "Only through education as one can receive in a cultural center can freedom become vitally important to men."

The beautiful building was originally "constructed to house the public library, a museum and an art gallery." The original project proposal stated:

The large building now housing city hall offices was originally built by the WPA between 1938 and 1940 for use as a Cultural Center, which included the public library. As city needs shifted, the building became home to city hall in 1946 and continues in that function today. *Courtesy of the Southeast Volusia Historical Society.*

"It is not contemplated that the property will be leased, sold, donated, or otherwise disposed of to a private individual or corporation or to a quasi-public organization, during the useful life of the improvements placed thereon through this project."

By October 1940, the public library had fully moved into the south wing of the center and housed over six thousand circulating books. The library contained all new furniture, which was produced through the use of WPA labor. The library operated much like a modern library does. There were regular operating hours, checkout limits, fines for overdue and damaged books and librarians available to help those with questions.

By the date of the formal dedication, the Cultural Center had grown to include the library, an art school, an exhibition gallery, a photographic dark room and a museum room, along with meeting space for culturally minded organizations. The building was so revolutionary that it is claimed First Lady

First Lady Eleanor Roosevelt is quoted as having very nice things to say about the New Smyrna Beach Cultural Center building. This building was constructed during the worst of the Great Depression using WPA funds. The building later held the library and city hall offices. The library moved to Riverside Drive in 1966. *Courtesy of the Library of Congress.*

Eleanor Roosevelt had this to say about it: "In New Smyrna Beach, they are dedicating a cultural center. They tell me it is the first building in the south to be erected for cultural purposes with funds from the WPA."

By the end of 1945, however, the world had changed, and art and culture were not the primary issues. World War II had sent millions of men to war, including many from New Smyrna Beach. Many of these were men who had been employed by organizations like the WPA. It was a different world after the war, and in November 1945, the New Smyrna Beach City Commission voted to take over the majority of space in the Cultural Center building starting on January 1, 1946.

This view is from between 1946 and 1966, when city hall and the public library shared the same building. This building was originally constructed as a Cultural Center. In 1966, the library moved to the Brannon Memorial Library located on Riverside Drive. *Courtesy of the author.*

By 1960, it was apparent that both the library and city hall needed more room. After much back and forth over cost, building design and more, the new Fred R. Brannon Jr. Library was opened in Riverside Park in December 1966. The library was named for the then recently deceased city attorney who had worked tirelessly for the cause of a new library.

City hall offices were then expanded to take over the entire WPA building. While the city has continued to grow, the main city government functions are still operating out of the same building.[28]

Located on the outside of city hall are several monuments varying in size, composition and noticeability. Sitting directly in front of the main entrance to the building is the Andrew Turnbull monument, which is discussed in further detail in this chapter under the "200th Anniversary Markers" heading. This is a coquina monument with a copper plaque honoring Turnbull and the men and women who helped settle the area.

Situated near the corner of Sams Avenue and Julia Street sits a purple and orange sculpture that serves a dual purpose. This one-of-a-kind piece of public art is titled *Garden Sculpture I* and is dated circa 1995. The artist is Doris Leeper.

The work, which is approximately one hundred inches tall and crafted out of aluminum, is both a reminder of the 125th anniversary of the incorporation of New Smyrna Beach (remember the incorporation date

Andrew Turnbull is memorialized at the front entry to city hall with a coquina and bronze monument. This monument pays tribute to Turnbull and the founding of the largest British colony in what was to become the United States. *Courtesy of the author.*

Garden Sculpture I, circa 1995, by artist Doris Leeper. Containing a purple base and red sphere on top, this sculpture incorporates simple shapes and basic colors to create a tension between balance and asymmetry. It is also the home to a time capsule that is to be opened in 2087. *Courtesy of the author.*

is different than the 1768 settlement date, when Andrew Turnbull and his indentured servants arrived) and also the primary marker for a time capsule that was dedicated and will be opened in 2087.

When discussing this important work by Ms. Leeper, then Stetson University professor Dr. James Murphy had this to say:

> *What I admire most about these late works by Doris Leeper are their precision, clarity and expressiveness. In* Garden Sculpture I, *she uses simple modules—in this case, three triangles and a sphere—to create a tension between balance and asymmetry, stability and implied movement, abstract form and figurative content. The sleek, epoxy paint surface of the sculpture complements the shapes, and also emphasizes her constant quest for dramatic high-tech effects.*

As for Ms. Leeper, Clay Henderson said, "She brought national recognition to New Smyrna Beach as an artist community and special attention to our unique environmental setting." Before her passing at age seventy-one, Ms. Leeper had become an internationally known sculptor and painter, with her works included in over one hundred collections. She moved to the New Smyrna Beach area in 1958 and lived in the ocean-side city of Eldora. Here she became involved in environmental movements and is often credited with being a leader in the formation of the Canaveral National Seashore. In addition, Ms. Leeper was the prime mover behind the 1977 founding and 1982 opening of the Atlantic Center for the Arts (ACA), located just north of New Smyrna Beach. The ACA is a sprawling campus of almost seventy acres with room for art of all types—painting, sculpture, dance, theater and more. Her activity in the ACA helped lead to the founding of the Alliance of Artists Communities, a grouping of similar artists' colonies that have a goal of supporting artists of all types. In 1999, Doris Leeper was enshrined in the Florida Artists Hall of Fame. Just to the north in Port Orange, a 1,637-acre nature preserve operated by Volusia County bears Doris Leeper's name—a beautiful tribute to a woman who did so much for the area.[29]

A small bronze on coquina monument sitting just to the left (south) of the main entrance to city hall commemorates the life of Lydia B. Pettis. Mrs. Pettis was a true humanitarian and gave selflessly to the community for the majority of her long life. Mrs. Pettis was born on January 28, 1899, and passed away on October 16, 1981. In those eighty-two years, she touched the lives of hundreds, if not thousands, of New Smyrna Beach's poor residents. While primarily known for her work in the African American community,

These bronze markers are on the ground next to the large abstract sculpture created by Doris Leeper that stands on city hall property. The marker nearest Sams Avenue and Julia Street is the plaque identifying the sculpture. On the opposite side is a plaque discussing the time capsule contained below the sculpture. *Courtesy of the author.*

she reached out to all, and the respect she garnered in the community appears to have known no limits.

The year 1929 was a pivotal one in the life of Mrs. Pettis. It was in that year that she founded the Christian Women's Alliance. This group was crucial in the building of what was to become the Minerva Monroe Library. This

Located near the front entry to city hall is a coquina and bronze memorial dedicated to the memory of Lydia Pettis. The monument pays tribute to Mrs. Pettis's many humanitarian efforts, in particular the Forgotten Christmas Tree. *Courtesy of the author.*

library, which catered to the needs of the African American community, also served as a meeting spot and gathering point for lectures, plays, concerts and religious meetings, all the while creating a positive impact on an untold number of citizens. The year also marked the beginning of what became a massive annual tradition in New Smyrna Beach: the Forgotten Christmas Tree, a program that ran continuously for fifty years. On the day after Christmas in 1929, Mrs. Pettis visited a sick neighbor who had no money for a doctor visit and only half a can of soup in her home to eat. Mrs. Pettis left the home but came back soon with food and medicine. She also made arrangements for a doctor's visit.

From those humble beginnings, the Forgotten Christmas Tree became a regular event in New Smyrna Beach. Each year, Mrs. Pettis and her volunteer group would begin asking local businesses for permission to place a box as a drop point for the event. It of course took time, but through the years support for the event grew, and more businesses and schools signed on as supporters.

Each year in the week following the official Christmas, an event was held, usually at the Minerva Monroe Library, where the contributions were distributed to needy members of the city. Adults and the elderly might receive clothing and a box of food, while children would receive toys and clothes. In the days leading up to the party, volunteers would carefully catalogue, wrap and organize the donations in order to make the greatest impact on recipients. The party became a large social event, and elected officials, community leaders and others would attend.

In addition to her charity works, Lydia Pettis was also a businesswoman. She operated a rooming house out of her home and, during the 1940s, a restaurant that was located on Washington Street.

During and after her life, Mrs. Pettis was given many honors for her charity works. In 1958, the national magazine *Sepia* ran an article describing the Forgotten Christmas Tree program and her other charitable works. On January 2, 1963, the city celebrated Lydia B. Pettis Appreciation Day, during which she was presented with a new car. The Southeast Volusia Chamber of Commerce awarded her a plaque inscribed, "Fifty Years of Community Caring." A large park located on Mary Avenue is named in her honor. This park includes basketball courts, tennis courts, a playground, picnic areas and more.

During May 1973, Mrs. Pettis received a special commendation from then president Richard Nixon. The certificate reads, "The President of the United States Awards this Commendation to Lydia Pettis in recognition of exceptional service to others, in the finest American tradition."

In a fitting remembrance to her life, the marker in front of city hall was dedicated on June 25, 1982. A transcript of Mayor George Musson's speech is included here as an appendix.[30]

There is a final small monument located near Julia Street to past mayor George Musson. Musson served as mayor an astounding nine terms from 1977 until 1995, when he passed away while still holding office. Musson was a lifelong resident of New Smyrna Beach and graduated from New Smyrna Beach High School before attending and graduating from the University of Florida. Musson was a veteran of the U.S. Army and served in Korea. In addition to local politics, Musson was a businessman and owned and operated Musson's Florist, a business started by his parents, for many years.

During his nearly two decades in office, Musson accomplished much. He is credited with a major role in the construction of the Harris Saxon high-rise bridge (commonly called the south bridge) and furthering the discussion that led to the widening of SR 44 to four lanes west of I-95. The George Musson Memorial Bridge (the northern bridge), opened in 1998 shortly after Musson's death, was named in his honor. The Musson Bridge has a span of twenty-one feet replacing the prior bridge, which allowed for only a fourteen-foot clearance. The bridge is opened three times an hour to allow for tall boat traffic to pass.

Connor Library Building

Those visiting the Old Fort Park area and seeing the beautifully restored and well taken care of building might have little understanding of the more than a century of history the building has seen.

Washington E. Connor was a wealthy New Yorker and member of the New York Stock Exchange who first visited New Smyrna in 1884 along with George Gould, the son of financier Jay Gould. In addition to acquiring over 3,000 acres of land, including the 450-acre Ronnoc Grove (Connor spelled backward), and also purchasing the land on which he and his wife believed an ancient Spanish mission once sat, he also constructed the New Smyrna Free Library in 1901 and financed its librarian as well.

Among Connor's other holdings was the Connor Bridge. This bridge would be considered the "north" bridge today. Working under the corporate name of New Smyrna Bridge and Investment Company, with $15,000 in capital, the toll bridge opened to great fanfare on March 4, 1894. Bridge tolls were one cent whether by vehicle, foot or bicycle. It is said that within eighteen days, the bridge provided a 10 percent return on the capital investment. While this estimate would mean that an unrealistic seventy-five thousand vehicles had crossed the bridge and returned to the mainland ($15,000 x .10 = $1,500; $1,500 ÷ $0.02 [toll to beachside and back] = 75,000 round trips across the bridge; 75,000 ÷ 18 days = 4,167 two-way trips per day), there can be little doubt that Connor's Bridge brought more traffic to the town of Coronado Beach.

By the early 1920s, however, the bridge was beginning to show considerable wear, and there was competition on the horizon in the form of a proposed south bridge. Connor, ever the businessman, offered a deal to the city. He proposed donating the library to the city if it agreed to purchase his bridge. The details for this agreement were finally hashed out after much back-and-forth discussion. New Smyrna took over operation of the Connor Library on July 1, 1924, with Marie Frost serving as librarian. During 1925, the state budgeted $32,500 for the purchase of the toll bridge.

In the deed transfer of the library building, there was a stipulation that years later would come back to cause the city an inordinate amount of difficulty. It was stated that the building could not be sold and that it was to remain a library. If the city did not uphold its end of the agreement, the property was to revert to Connor heirs. Despite this, in 1941 the library was moved into a WPA-constructed building known as the New Smyrna Beach Cultural Center—or, as we know it today, city hall. In the years after

A small bronze monument now marks the location at the southeast corner of the United Church of Christ. The Connor Library building stood on this property until March 1991, when it was moved to Old Fort Park. It has since been used as meeting space, the first home for the New Smyrna Museum of History and, most recently, the Community Redevelopment Agency. *Courtesy of the author.*

the move, the local Garden Club used the building and included a small collection of books to keep up the appearance of a library.

The Connor Library was originally located on the corner of Faulkner and Washington Streets. Today, this lot is part of the property owned by the United Church of Christ. A small marker now signifies where the building used to stand.

The original library for New Smyrna was three hundred volumes donated by Mr. Connor and housed in the narthex of the United Church of Christ. The popularity of the library soon made this small area unacceptable, and after a short while, it was housed in a small building located near where the current Masonic lodge stands until a more permanent home was built by Mr. Connor near the corner of Faulkner and Washington Streets. The dedication of the building in October 1901 was quite a party. It is said that a bonfire lit the grounds and Japanese lanterns hung across the front of the building. A library committee, with Mayor C.G. Hesse serving as chairman, was appointed. Mr. Connor financed the library and paid for the librarian for more than twenty years.

By 1981, several organizations had staked out claims on the building and the land on which it sat. The building was in need of repairs, and who would pay for those repairs was in doubt. The adjacent United Church of Christ was interested in the land, saying the building had become an eyesore. The Garden Club wanted to continue using the building and offered to make the needed repairs if the city could guarantee it occupancy. Connor heir Mrs. John W. Bitner also had interest in the property based on the original contract provisions. By 1987, things had changed little except for the city claiming that all Connor heirs could not be located. A new player, however, was beginning to enter the game: the Southeast Volusia Historical Society and its president, George Wolsfelt, then owner of the Alba Court Inn. While neither entity owned the property, both had strong views about what should be done with it. The church requested a quitclaim deed to the title and suggested giving the building to the historical society if it was willing to find a new home for it and restore it. Wolsfelt, however, believed the building could have stayed where it was and been restored there. Larry Sweett may have said it best at a historical commission meeting: "We must get a plan, establish what we as a group want to do. We'd better get our act together or there will be a pile of rubble there without even a cross to commemorate what used to be there." Both plans, however, hinged on the city having clear title to the building. That was still in question.

By November 1987, still without clear plans in place concerning usage or even where the building would be located, the Southeast Volusia Historical Society began a fundraising campaign called "Save the Historic Connor Library." According to Doug Davich, a contractor and historic preservation board member, the cost to restore the building would be around $30,000 to $40,000. By the time all was said and done, this estimate was grossly inadequate.

As 1988 passed, there was still indecision about the corner property and the Connor Library. In February, the city filed suit to obtain clear title to the property. In the meantime, the local historic preservation board put forth several uses for a restored building, including storage, historic displays or use as a meeting facility. The United Church of Christ continued to have interest in the small lot as well.

Progress was made later in 1988, when an agreement was put into place with the city, the United Church of Christ and Connor family heirs. The city would become the owner of the lot and building, which would then be sold to the church for $22,000. These funds would be used to move and rehabilitate the building. If the library could not be saved, the funds were to be used for other restoration projects as dictated by the Historic New Smyrna

Beach Preservation Commission. There was to be no future building on the site where the library had once sat. Lastly, the church was required to place a monument on the site outlining the role of the Connor family in the history of New Smyrna Beach.

While all looked rosy, it wasn't going to be that easy. The issue of property title was still tied up in the legal system. There was still the issue of where the building would be moved to in addition to where the additional money was going to come from for the cost of moving and restoration. The $22,000 was going to be approximately one-sixth of the final total.

In the months that followed, it was proposed that the building be moved to Old Fort Park. In October, however, the Historic Preservation Commission was again waffling and voted three to one, with three members absent, to recommend that the building be moved to the small park across the street from 120 Sams Avenue (120 Sams Avenue is where the New Smyrna Museum of History is now located, and the suggested park area would later become Emory Bennett Park).

It wasn't until March 1990 that momentum really began to pick up on the project. On March 22, circuit court judge James T. Nelson signed the final agreement granting the city title to the land and building. This set in motion the rest of the agreed-upon stipulations. The church put a down payment of $4,600 on the property, with the balance due thirty days after the property was moved. The city had one year to remove the building or the church, at its discretion, would be allowed to move or demolish the building at the expense of the city. Around this time, a final destination for the building was decided on: the southwest corner of Old Fort Park. Final zoning approval for the move was granted in July. In October, the Southeast Volusia Historical Society agreed to help raise funds, labor and materials for the renovation. Society board member Harold Cardwell had this to say at the time: "If this goes through, and I'm sure it will, it's the best thing that's ever happened to New Smyrna."

With many of the details now attended to, city officials began the work of having the building moved. Larue House Movers and Sons was awarded a $26,141 contract to move the library, and on March 7, 1991, the short move was completed and excitement was high. Carol Kerrigan of the Preservation Commission said, "To me, it just looks perfect in there, and I just can't wait until we get it fixed up. I wasn't sure how it would look there at first, but it fits right in." Despite the excitement, there was the reality of raising money still looming. The $30,000 to $40,000 estimate of a few years earlier was, by June, in the $150,000 range. Grant funding was coming in, though, and word of a $25,000 matching state grant kept spirits high.

After many years of neglect and back-and-forth arguments, the Connor Library building was moved from its original home on the corner of Washington and Faulkner Streets to a more central location in Old Fort Park. *Courtesy of the Southeast Volusia Historical Society.*

Fundraising efforts by the Southeast Volusia Historical Society included a Carolina-style barbecue. The society also agreed to provide funding for outside streetlights and for the deadbolt locks on the doors. Society volunteers also helped with painting and other repair work in anticipation of taking over the day-to-day maintenance once the building was complete.

By April 1992, work had begun, including fumigation for termites. Work on the building included a new roof, removal of old paint, painting all areas, opening the outside porches to return the building to its original look, adding air conditioning and more, including a new "New Smyrna Free Library" sign that replicated the original that hung over the front steps.

On Wednesday, October 14, 1992, the Connor Library was unveiled to more than one hundred onlookers who were eager to see the fruits of years of labor. Mayor George Musson served as master of ceremonies and introduced many of the dignitaries in attendance. During his remarks, county

After sitting empty for many years, a short move and then further waiting, the Connor Library was lovingly restored and unveiled to the public in 1992. It has since served as meeting space, a home for the New Smyrna Museum of History and, most recently, the Community Redevelopment Agency. *Courtesy of the author.*

councilman Clay Henderson had this to say: "How do you save history? You do it one building at a time. This is a wonderful start."

Once complete, the project's cost of approximately $120,000 had been financed through several sources: $51,300 from the Florida Department of State, Division of Historical Resources; $41,700 from the city; $25,000 in Community Redevelopment Agency (CRA) funds; and $2,000 from the Southeast Volusia Historical Society. This total does not include the value of in-kind services.

In addition to the local praise and accolades, the work that was completed received wider recognition. In May 1993, architect Keith C. Hock, Herwald Construction and the City of New Smyrna Beach were awarded an Outstanding Award for Nonresidential Restoration in Florida from the Florida Trust for Historic Preservation.

In the years that have followed its renovation, the Connor Library building has served several functions. It has served as home to displays from the Southeast Volusia Historical Society. While smaller in size than the current museum, this set of displays was an important step in validating the need for a full-sized history museum in the area. In February 1999, the building

The Historic New Smyrna Beach Historic Property Plaque Program allows property owners to purchase bronze plaques denoting their properties' historic nature. Participation in this program is voluntary and does not diminish a property owner's rights. As of this writing, there are forty properties participating. One participating property is scheduled for demolition. Historic property number one, as shown here, is the Connor Library. *Courtesy of the author.*

was the focal point of a new historic marker program instituted by the city. This program is the Historic Property Plaque Program. Property owners may submit an application to purchase one of the bronze plaques. After receiving approval from the Historic New Smyrna Beach Preservation Commission and paying the appropriate fee, owners will receive a numbered plaque that is to be affixed near the front entrance of the building. This program does not infringe on a property owner's future rights; rather, it signifies the historic nature and value of a home. The Connor Library was issued plaque number one.

By 1996, however, the building had become too small for the growing Southeast Volusia Historical Society, and it began to look elsewhere. The city agreed and began negotiating with the society to lease or sell the building located just south at 120 Sams Avenue—the old post office, as it was commonly known.

By 2002, a deal had been struck, and with the historical society now in a different building, the Connor Library was again vacant. The building was used as meeting space and also housed a consulting group that was working to develop the CRA master plan. In 2009, with the CRA in full operation, it was moved to the building and remained there until the spring of 2015.[31]

200TH ANNIVERSARY MARKERS

There are actually two monuments dedicated to the 200th anniversary of New Smyrna Beach. Sitting near the sidewalk facing Sams Avenue, under stately oak trees and often hidden due to parked cars, sits an important monument in the history of New Smyrna Beach: the coquina monument known as *To the Past…To the Present…To the Future* or, more commonly, the New Smyrna bicentennial monument. This is not a memorial to all those who arrived in the New World with Dr. Andrew Turnbull; rather, it is a monument placed by the American Hellenic Educational Progressive Association (AHEPA) to commemorate the "Intrepid Hellenes" who were part of the settlement. A second monument sits almost directly across Sams Avenue near the entryway to city hall. This is a monument to Dr. Andrew Turnbull, the founder of the largest British colony in the New World.

The settling of New Smyrna in 1768 brought people of many nationalities, including around four hundred Greeks. For the 200th anniversary of New Smyrna (then Beach) in 1968, the AHEPA, the Jane Sheldon Chapter of the DAR and the city pulled out all the stops in a large celebration held in Old Fort Park.

The AHEPA can trace its roots to Atlanta in 1922, when a group of eight men of Greek descent came together to form a fraternity dedicated to improving the image of Greeks and to helping those from Greece assimilate into American society. The organization has evolved and now has a mission of Hellenism (a devotion to ancient Greek thought, styles or customs), education, philanthropy, civic responsibility and personal excellence. The Daytona Beach lodge was established in January 1962.

Also playing a role in the celebration was the local DAR chapter. The Daughters of the American Revolution come from a variety of backgrounds and interests but all share a common bond of having an ancestor who helped contribute to securing the independence of the United States of America. This is a nondenominational group, and any woman with a direct lineal line to a Revolutionary War soldier is eligible to apply for admission. The Jane Sheldon Chapter of New Smyrna Beach has been active since October 1925.[32]

Zelia W. Sweett was the leading historian of New Smyrna Beach for many years. She was the founder of the Jane Sheldon Chapter of the Daughters of the American Revolution. Here she stands with the flag of New Smyrna Beach. This flag is now on display at the New Smyrna Museum of History. *Courtesy of Zelia V. Sweett.*

The New Smyrna Beach Bicentennial Committee consisted of Mayor Robert C. Patillo, E.E. Hughes, Corita Doggett Corse, Mrs. Harris Saxon, Mrs. Maccie Smith, Hannah D. Bonnet, Mrs. Joe Gilliam, Laurence W. Galbreath, Richard D. Paxton, Jack Scarborough, Edwin G. Whitney, Mrs. F. Russell Galbreath and Zelia Sweett. These dedicated men and women helped put together what was "expected to be the largest crowd of visitors at any New Smyrna Beach event."

The events of the day were divided in two, with a luncheon at the yacht club serving as the dividing point. The morning of May 4, 1968, started early, with coffee provided by the DAR at the Masonic lodge located across Washington Street from Old Fort Park and city hall. The event was started with an invocation given by Reverend Cannon Dorsey G. Smith Jr. of St. James Episcopal Church of Ormond Beach. The New Smyrna Beach High School band, under the direction of Barbara Muller, then played several numbers, with guitar solos by Valerie Wilson and Ms. Muller and an accordion solo by Ronnie Luznar. All soloists performed in costumes representing what the original settlers might have worn.

The New Smyrna Yacht Club was established in 1928. The private club now features dining, tennis, swimming and more. The club is located just south of the downtown area. *Courtesy of the author.*

The ceremony leader was Judge Robert H. Wingfield. He introduced the many local dignitaries attending the event, all of whom were greeted by New Smyrna Beach mayor Robert C. Pattillo. Bransford Littleton, a member of American Legion Post 17, gave the salute to the flag. He was followed by Kenneth H. Beeson. Mr. Beeson was a descendant from one of the original Minorcan settlers in New Smyrna and was a noted authority on St. Augustine and Minorcan history. He was a founding member of the Minorcan Cultural Society and taught for many years in the St. Johns River Community College History Department. His talk discussed Dr. Andrew Turnbull as an eighteenth-century individual and founder of the city.

After Dr. Beeson's talk, Eileen Butts took center stage in order to present the plaque and monument to the City of New Smyrna Beach. Two young descendants from the original settlement—Walter Mulbry, a descendant of Dr. Turnbull, and Debra Lyn Meares, a descendant of colonists with the surname Rogero, Mestre and Lopez—unveiled the coquina monument with a bronze plaque. The plaque reads:

Dr. Andrew Turnbull
Dec. 2, 1720–March 13, 1792
Founder of the largest colony

under British rule ever
to come to the New World. The
New Smyrna Colony of Florida
1768–1778
Placed by the
Volusia County Historical Commission
1968

After the presentation of the monument, Father Edward Coyne, rector of Sacred Heart Catholic Church, gave the benediction.

At 1:00 p.m., the city had a lunch scheduled at the nearby yacht club. Here, members of the Florida Historical Society, who were meeting in Daytona, along with local, county and state dignitaries and members of the AHEPA, dined with the then arriving governor of Florida, Claude Kirk, who flew in especially for the event.

Florida governor Claude Kirk was the first Republican elected to the seat since Reconstruction. He served as thirty-sixth governor of the state from 1967 to 1971. In 1968, he visited New Smyrna Beach to take part in the city's bicentennial celebration. *Courtesy of the State Archives of Florida.*

After lunch, it was back to Old Fort Park for another monument dedication. At 3:00 p.m., the dedication of the monument placed by the AHEPA began. Special guests included Andrew Fasseas, supreme president of the Order of AHEPA; Metropolitan Germanos from New York, representing the Greek Orthodox Church; Joanna Panagopoulos from the Daughters of Penelope, AHEPA Auxiliary; and James Schofield, chairman of the National AHEPA Bicentennial Celebration. They were joined by AHEPA dignitaries, local leaders and Governor Kirk. After the monument dedication, there was a Greek *glendi*—a festival featuring singing, dancing and

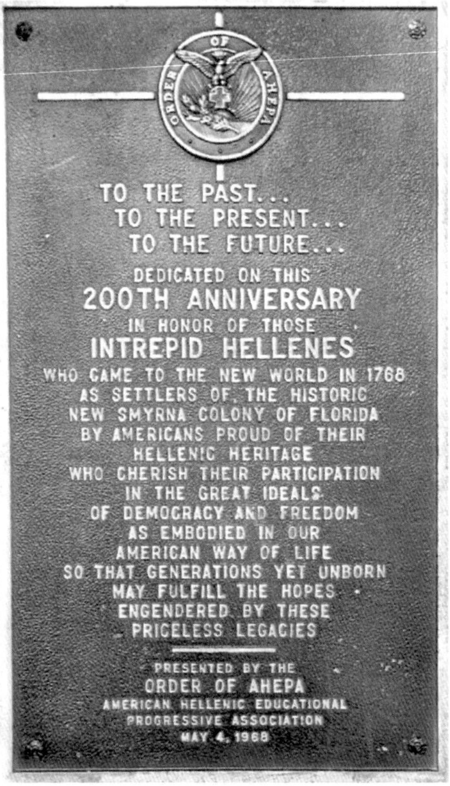

A close-up of the bronze plaque placed in 1968 by the AHEPA to commemorate the 200th anniversary of the settlement of Smyrna. The monument is specifically dedicated to the Intrepid Hellenes, or Greeks, who were part of the settlement. *Courtesy of the author.*

food that lasted well into the early evening hours.

The monument continues to be a draw for Greeks, and there have been memorial services there in the past to commemorate the Greek settlers who helped found New Smyrna. During a service in 1988, city commissioner Doug Davich had this to say: "It's always a pleasure to see the Greek people celebrating [by] their Plymouth Rock."

The inscription on the marker reads:

To the past…
To the present…
To the future…
Dedicated on this
200th ANNIVERSARY
in honor of those
INTREPID HELLENES
who came to the new world in 1768
as settlers of the historic
New Smyrna colony of Florida
by Americans proud of the
Hellenic heritage
who cherish their participation
in the great ideals

of democracy and freedom
as embodied in our
American way of life
so that generations yet unborn
may fulfill the hopes
engendered by these
priceless legacies.
Presented by the
ORDER OF AHEPA
American Hellenic Educational
Progressive Association
May 4, 1968[33]

Chamber of Commerce Building

At the far eastern end of Canal Street on the north side sits the chamber of commerce building. This grand building has undergone some physical changes over the years but has stayed in the same location since the building was constructed using Civil Works Administration funds during the Great Depression.

The current Southeast Volusia Chamber of Commerce can trace its origins back to a local board of trade that was active in 1915. By 1926, the chamber was a known entity, but the first formal charter was not approved until 1932. The chamber charter proclaimed a goal of "promotion of civic, economic, and social welfare of the people of New Smyrna and vicinity." At this time, the chamber was renting space from H.H. Sams in a building very close to where the chamber now resides. With the Great Depression raging, federal funding was being made available in an effort to help put people to work and jumpstart the economy. The chamber building would become one of these projects.

In January 1915, with the Great War continuing in Europe, a group of business and professional men arranged a social dinner at the Alba Court Inn with the goal of allowing businessmen and winter visitors an opportunity to become acquainted. Sixty-six people took advantage of the opportunity and formed an organization that one hundred years later still has a major role in local business, politics and social activities.

This group originally called itself the One Circle Club and later changed the name to the Men's Club. Its aim was "extending our acquaintances to promote the spirit of fraternity and good fellowship among men and to advance the interest of the City of New Smyrna." In taking the pledge to this group, members swore to "be a man and treat every other man as a brother." Member dues were $1.50 per person, and members could be expelled for dishonesty, intemperance or gross immorality.

Postwar years were a boom, and the fledgling chamber was booming alongside the economy. A large membership drive was started, and a pledge drive of $50,000 was begun. The City of New Smyrna backed this drive and contributed $10,000. By the end of January, the goal had been achieved, and there were over two thousand paying members of the chamber. With success in hand, chamber president John H. Hibbard proclaimed, "We shall promote civic, economic and social welfare of the people of New Smyrna and the vicinity."

These same words were included in the first charter that was adopted in July 1932 during the height of the Great Depression. By September 1932, it was asked by new chamber president F.D. Bristley that all out-of-work individuals register at the chamber. His goal was to be able to put as many men to work as possible once federal relief arrived.

From more than two thousand members in 1926, membership had crashed to only eighty-six by 1933. The chamber was still residing in rented quarters, and the future looked cloudy.

December 1933 brought some positive news to New Smyrna amid all the doom and gloom. Chamber president Bristley revealed that negotiations were underway to obtain public works funding. The *Daily News* was reporting on the likelihood of a new chamber of commerce building. In anticipation, the city acquired title to the building site.

It was shortly learned that approximately $18,500 had been approved through the Civil Works Administration for the project. In addition to enlarging the chamber building, it was moved approximately fifty feet and turned in order to face Canal Street. The major additions to the property included a "lounging room" on the first floor and an auditorium on the second floor.

In addition to the chamber building, repairs were made at local schools using CWA funds. These jobs proved a godsend to local workers; carpenters earned sixty cents an hour, masons earned eighty cents an hour, electricians earned seventy-five cents an hour, roofers earned eighty cents an hour and plumbers and superintendents were paid one dollar per hour. For men who were out of work, these were welcome opportunities.

The work was completed quickly, and in January 1934, chamber president Bristley set the dedication date for the improved building: March 3, 1934. The CWA was a short-lived program and was closed in March 1934. Other

The chamber of commerce has always been a leader in local business affairs. This photo dates from 1955–60, as is evidenced by the banner welcoming Governor Leroy Collins. In more recent years, the building has been returned to look more like its original state. It is now also home to the Artists' Workshop. *Courtesy of the Southeast Volusia Historical Society.*

federal programs such as the WPA helped to keep men working and money flowing as the country struggled to regain its footing.

In the years after the Great Depression and World War II, the chamber of commerce has kept active and played a vital role in New Smyrna Beach. The chamber has been a key promoter of the city and has helped attract visitors from across the continent, with outreach to Canadians being a prime goal. Stabilization of the Ponce Inlet jetty, a modern bridge building, the creation of four lanes on Highway 44 and the purchasing of land for what was to become the Canaveral National Seashore are some of the chamber's highlights.

The year 2012 saw the outside of the chamber building restored and the roof repaired. Community Redevelopment Agency funding was used to help update and modernize bathrooms, the boardroom and the vestibule area. Other repairs and upgrades to lighting, flooring and the original coquina structure were made as well. For its efforts, the chamber was recognized for Outstanding Achievement in Restoration/Rehabilitation by the Florida Trust for Historic Preservation.

Today, the chamber is a major force in the promotion of New Smyrna Beach. In addition to promoting business, it offers relocation services, tourist information and other services. A small paid staff, a loyal group of volunteers and an active board are carrying on the work of men like F.D. Bristley, John D. DeBerry, Henry C. Swoope, T.C. Wilder and others in order to keep the chamber a relevant and leading piece of the New Smyrna Beach landscape.[34]

THE MARY S. HARRELL BLACK HERITAGE MUSEUM

Located on the west side of the railroad tracks downtown on Duss Street sits the Mary S. Harrell Black Heritage Museum. This fine museum is located in what was once the St. Rita's Colored Catholic Mission building.

The small church building was constructed in 1899 as Sacred Heart Catholic Church. In 1956, the building was relocated from its original location on Faulkner Street to its present site in the historically black Westside neighborhood. The local diocese relocated the building with the goal of enlarging the African American Catholic population. Building preservation was a secondary reason for the move. The building was renamed St. Rita's Colored Catholic Mission after it was moved.

Father Raymond Schantz served as priest and conducted the first Mass held in the newly relocated church. Over the next years, there were several other priests: James Murphy, Thomas Radley, Francis Salmon and Francis Walsh.

During the 1960s, the entire country was changing. Integration was the reality in schools, businesses and churches. Sacred Heart Catholic Church was integrated in 1969, and the St. Rita's Mission was converted into a clinic and daycare facility sponsored by the Southeast Volusia Democratic Women's Club. The building served in this capacity for nearly twenty years before being abandoned in the late 1980s. The church intended to use the property for a heritage center and as a location for public meetings, but those plans never came to pass. The condition of the building continued to deteriorate, and the city threatened to take down the building that meant so much to the African American Catholic community.

Longtime resident and retired educator Mary S. Harrell and her husband, Jimmy, led the efforts to preserve the structure. Through the efforts of the Harrells, the Old Sacred Heart/St. Rita's Restoration Committee was formed. This dedicated group worked with the City of New Smyrna Beach and other organizations to begin saving the building.

First named Sacred Heart Catholic Church, this building was later moved to its current location and renamed St. Rita's Colored Catholic Mission. After integration, the building was a daycare and, after years of neglect, was sold to the Black Heritage Festival of New Smyrna Beach. It is now home to the Mary S. Harrell Black Heritage Museum. *Courtesy of the Southeast Volusia Historical Society.*

As always in a project like this, funding was the issue. In 1997, the committee received a $27,500 grant from the Bureau of Historic Preservation, and in 1999 an additional $70,000 grant was awarded. Also in 1999, the Catholic Diocese of Orlando deeded the property to the nonprofit organization the Black Heritage Festival of New Smyrna Beach. These grants, along with funds raised by locals and through the Diocese of Orlando, allowed work to begin. The members of the Black Heritage Festival of New Smyrna Beach, led by Mrs. Harrell, along with the architectural and contracting firm Williamson Dacar, had the restoration work completed and displays installed and finally opened the Black Heritage Museum in December. The name of the museum was changed in 2012 to reflect the tireless efforts of Mary S. Harrell.[35]

Today, visitors to the museum can learn about the legacy provided by African Americans not just to New Smyrna Beach but also to our entire country. Displays include discussions about slavery with a display showing what an Underground Railroad quilt would have looked like, an assortment of inventions by African Americans, the Florida East Coast Railway, stories of local residents and much more.

The Mary S. Harrell Black Heritage Museum building was constructed in 1899 as Sacred Heart Catholic Church. In 1956, the building was moved to its current location and became the St. Rita's Colored Catholic Mission. In 1999, the property was deeded to the Black Heritage Festival of New Smyrna Beach and now houses a museum. *Courtesy of the author.*

It is impossible to discuss the museum without telling a brief snippet about the woman whose name adorns the building. Mrs. Harrell was born on March 27, 1933, in Bainbridge, Georgia. Bainbridge is located in the southwest corner of the state in Decatur County. When Mary was born, the town had a population of fewer than six thousand, and today it is still only around thirteen thousand strong. The town was named for U.S. Navy commodore William Bainbridge. Mrs. Harrell earned her AA degree from Gibbs Junior College (which in 1965 merged with St. Petersburg Junior College and is now called St. Petersburg College) and a BS degree from Bethune-Cookman College. Religion played an important role in her life, and she was a member of the Allen Chapel AME Church. She worked for more than thirty years for the Volusia County School Board, retiring in 1995. Mrs. Harrell passed away in August 2014.[36]

The legacy being carried out at this museum by Jimmy Harrell may best be summed up in the words of former New Smyrna Beach city commissioner Oretha Bell: "St. Rita's is the reference point for our community." She continued, "We are proud to have this wealth of information about our local history available to our youngsters. Our history was left out of the books."[37]

4
Riverside Drive

All the rivers run into the sea; yet the sea is not full.
—King Solomon

A trip along Riverside Drive (the road that used to be Hillsboro Street) is a chance to take your time and enjoy the beauty that truly is New Smyrna Beach. On the east is the beautiful Indian River, and on the west are some well-maintained homes, including several that are now bed-and-breakfast businesses. In addition, there are several historic sites that you will see along the way.

New Smyrna Lodge Number 149, Free and Accepted Masons of Florida

Sitting just across Washington Avenue from Old Fort Park is a large, well-kept building that is home to Mason Lodge 149. While having received their charter in 1896, the Masons did not move into their current home until 1927. In the thirty years prior to the opening of their temple, the Masons met at eight other locations in the downtown New Smyrna area.

On January 23, 1896, Florida Grand Lodge officers announced that the New Smyrna Lodge had been granted its charter and was assigned number 149. It was then that fifteen master Masons and one entered apprentice

This view is from the north causeway looking west toward the downtown area. Easily viewable are the Masonic lodge and the water tower then located in Old Fort Park. The building in front of the water tower is no longer in existence. *Courtesy of the author.*

began freemasonry in New Smyrna. They originally met in the second floor of the C.L. Dohn Feed Store, located on the corner of Canal and Faulkner Streets. During the first ten years of existence, only five men held the title of worshipful master. On October 13, 1905, the Dohn Feed Store burned to the ground, destroying all property owned by the Masons. For the next twenty-one years, the Masons met at seven other locations, all the while making plans for their own permanent temple.

In August 1925, the land on the corner of Washington and Hillsboro (now Riverside Drive) was purchased for $15,000. A building committee went to work, and in February 1926, it submitted plans for a temple. By May, bids were being accepted, and the bid from Donald F. Douglas in the amount of $51,433 was the winner. In June 1927, it was agreed that the building would be 102 feet long, 50 feet wide and 42 feet tall. The building was to be recessed from the front property line by 81 feet.

December 1927 was a joyous time for local Masons. The first meetings were held in the new temple, and on December 30, a formal dedication was held with an address given by senior grand warden Stafford Caldwell. Afterward, the installation of Lennon Guy Jordan as worshipful master was held. By May 1928, a complete financial picture of the temple was possible: land, $15,000; architect, $1,043; and contractor, $53,479. Though now in debt $20,000, the Masons owned their own building and

The corner of what are now Riverside Drive and Washington Street is shown here in this 1927 photo. Construction is about to start, and workers are warned "No Loafing," according to the sign attached to what appears to be the construction office. Builder Donald F. Douglas completed construction in less than six months. *Courtesy of the Southeast Volusia Historical Society.*

were no longer at the whim of landlords who could evict or raise rent with little notice.

The next decade became a mixed bag for the local lodge. Membership had risen to 240 in 1929 and 250 in 1930, and former worshipful master Donald F. Douglas was appointed district deputy grand master. Temple ownership, however, led to increased costs such as electric, water, telephone, maintenance, insurance and taxes. As the Great Depression clamped down on citizens, the lodge began to feel the effects as well. Many were unable to find work and could not pay their dues, and meeting attendance was dropping. By 1934, membership had declined to 164 despite dues being lowered.

There were great concerns about the mortgage on the temple. The original balance of $20,000 had been paid down to only $19,200 in seven years. Secretary Herbert E. Donnelly met with the mortgage holder, Mr.

William J. Statter Carr, and he agreed to several terms that were favorable to the Masons. The mortgage was cut to $15,000, $1,445 in back interest was forgiven, no interest would be charged on $5,000 of the loan, the interest on the remaining balance would be cut from 7 to 5 percent and a revised payment schedule was created. These generous changes allowed the Masons to keep current despite a continued slide in membership and other effects of the Depression.

Members of the lodge were active during World War II, and things began to slowly turn around locally. War bonds were purchased, a new roof was installed and by the time the lodge turned fifty in 1946, membership had rebounded to over two hundred. Through donations and bequests, the mortgage was being paid ahead of schedule, and in 1951 a campaign was started to raise the final $3,500 needed to clear this debt. In November, the goal was met with the assistance of the Order of the Eastern Star auxiliary, and on December 27, 1951, a large party was held to commemorate the event. State senator E. William Gautier was the lead speaker. The widow of Herbert Donnelly did the honors of burning the mortgage papers.

In 1953 and 1954, the lodge partnered with the city in building the new north causeway bridge. The lodge donated land from the front of its property in return for sidewalks being placed along Riverside Drive and Washington Street adjacent to the building.

The 1950s and '60s appear to have been a stable and positive time for members. Member growth appears to have been steady, and upgrades to the building were the norm. Upgrades such as a sound system, air conditioning, paint and routine maintenance were handled. By 1970, membership had reached a high of almost four hundred before starting a slow decline.

Also associated with the building is the Order of the Eastern Star Chapter #3. The Order of the Eastern Star can trace its origins to the mid-1800s, when Rob and Charlotte Morris decided to start an organization that allowed master Masons and their spouses to participate in the Masonic life together. While the Masons are men only, the Eastern Star has traditionally been aimed more toward women, though master Masons may join.

The twenty founding ladies of the New Smyrna chapter were first granted a charter on May 4, 1898, and the chapter was originally known as Dolores #7. The chapter was named for the daughter of Mr. and Mrs. J.M. Boyette. In the beginning, the chapter was under jurisdiction of the grand patron of Alabama. It would stay that way until 1904, when the Florida Grand Chapter was formed. New Smyrna members Minnie Moore and Nettie V. Turner were elected grand conductress and grand adah, respectively.

The New Smyrna Beach Masonic Lodge can trace its roots to 1896. In the years following, the group met at several locations before starting construction in 1927. The lodge was complete and the first meeting was held in December 1927. Today, the lodge has a nice blue and white exterior and is still home to the Masons almost ninety years later. *Courtesy of the author.*

Nettie Turner held several posts of great responsibility until 1907, when she was elected grand matron. Nettie had an active year leading the order. She oversaw the organization of six new chapters and a gain of 150 new members. At the twelfth triennial Assembly of the General Grand Chapter, Nettie was appointed worthy grand organist, the first Grand Chapter appointee from Florida. In addition, Nettie also recommended that Florida chapters be renumbered to reflect the order in which they were chartered. Because some chapters had disbanded, the Dolores #7 became known as Dolores #3 in 1909. The chapter was to change its name again in 1923, when it became known as New Smyrna #3.

The Great Depression was a difficult time not just for the Masons but also for the New Smyrna #3 chapter. In 1929, there was a problem with the check that was written to the Grand Chapter for dues. Many banks had closed, and the local ladies ultimately had to re-raise the funds in order to make sure their dues were paid and the chapter could stay open. As the economy continued to be dormant, the local treasurer absconded with much of the chapter's money, forcing it to accept a payment from the Grand Chapter to keep it afloat.

Times would change, however, and the New Smyrna Chapter #3's fortunes would improve greatly. During World War II, the chapter was an active purchaser of war bonds. In the postwar era, the chapter has continued its charity work in addition to supporting the lodge. Funds have been raised for projects as diverse as roof and elevator repairs to sending funds to the Grand Chapter in New Jersey to assist victims of Hurricane Sandy.

The Masons and the Order of the Eastern Star continue to be vibrant and active organizations in New Smyrna Beach despite many other opportunities for men and women to join other fraternal organizations. Their members are active in many other civic organizations and businesses. They meet regularly at the lodge, which sits proudly on the northwest corner of Washington Street and Riverside Drive just before or after crossing the north bridge, depending on which way you are traveling.[38]

"Old Fort" Ruins

Is it a fort? Is it a basement? Is it the foundation for the Turnbull Palace? Archaeologists have puzzled over this location for years. Locals have created their own stories and myths as well, all leading to a somewhat confusing story that ultimately has no 100 percent agreed-upon conclusion. For those looking for a definitive answer here, you will be disappointed. Rather, we will briefly discuss people we know for certain have owned the property and what they did with it.

Included at the ruins are the remains of an Indian midden that was excavated briefly in 1989 by Dana St. Clair and others at the request of the City of New Smyrna Beach in order to assess possibly repairing and strengthening a WPA-added wall at the ruins. His analysis was:

> *The midden is composed of initially densely packed and at greater depths relatively loosely packed oyster with some clam. There were occasional pockets of murex and razor clam, as well as concentrations of clam*

Opposite, bottom: The myth of the "Old Fort" is one that persists despite a lack of evidence that the structure was ever used as such. During the Civil War, a hotel owned by the Sheldon family stood on the site and was bombed by the Union navy. The ruins are now owned by the City of New Smyrna Beach and are part of what is called Old Fort Park. *Courtesy of the author.*

The mysterious ruins located in Old Fort Park have been called many things such as a fort and the ruins of Turnbull's Palace, as shown in this photo featuring Zelia Sweett on the left. It is known that the Sheldon family owned a building that sat on top of the ruins. This was often used as a hotel and, in 1863, was destroyed by the Union navy. *Courtesy of the Southeast Volusia Historical Society.*

> *(quahog). Faunal materials were abundant throughout...* [and] *were mainly fish, including mullet, stingray, shark, and redfish as identifiable species. Turtle was often seen. Also observed was deer, crab, rabbit, birds, and several unidentified small mammals. As a general observation fish remains increased from lower to higher levels.*[39]

Based on these findings, the midden has been primarily dated to the St. Johns II period, or approximately AD 800 through AD 1650. There were findings from the earlier St. Johns I period, but the majority of trash was from the later period. These findings—and thus dates—rule out the possibility that the midden was built around and over the ruins.

The ruins themselves are made of coquina. It is generally rectangular in shape, with the west wall being one foot longer than the east wall. The north and south walls are the same measurement. The interior is divided by parallel walls that cross, thus creating the various chambers or rooms that modern visitors see. In the 1930s, WPA workers added to the ruins by the "construction of several retaining walls, the reconstruction of one of the interior foundation walls, the restoration and reconstruction of a considerable portion of a low building wall around the perimeter and reconstruction of some of the steps in the north and south additions."[40]

It is known that by 1805, Ambrose Hull, who had earlier received a two-thousand-acre grant from the Spanish government, was in the process of building a home, and he had masons working to build "a small airy stone house of two stories, with necessary outhouse of the same material, which will probably be completed in the course of the next month." Hull later wrote to relatives, "Our house is situated upon a delightful hill surrounded with olives...Our house is built with hewn stone two stories—In the main body of the house are two large rooms one above the other—three double doors and six windows in each."[41]

The Hull plantation was short-lived, however, and in 1812 it was destroyed in what was known as the Patriots War. In 1830, Hull's heirs sold the land to Mary Dunham and the group of William DePeyster and Henry Cruger. DePeyster and Cruger, who were to begin construction on a sugar mill to the west of town the same year, built a house on the property that would later be occupied by the Sheldon family. As Jane Sheldon recounted later:

> *On May 8th 1832 I was married to John Dwight Sheldon, and in October 1835, removed with him and my mother to New Smyrna. Mr. Sheldon was placed in charge of the Cruger and Depyete* [sic] *property, in the*

absence of their manager, occupying their resident on the Hill, known as the Turnbull Castle.

By 1840, the home was gone, presumably destroyed during the Christmas 1835 Seminole Indian attack.[42]

The property was later sold to Thomas Stamps, who in turn sold the property to John Sheldon. The Sheldon house was described by son Rhodolphus:

My father, John Dwight Sheldon, had finished the house in 1850, and opened it as a tavern. It was a large structure of about sixty rooms, built of dressed lumber from the north, brought on their return voyages by the schooners that carried live oak timber north, and was the largest and best built house of entertainment south of St. Augustine.[43]

In 1863, the Union navy, which knew Mosquito Inlet was a favorite of blockade-runners, opened fire, destroying the home and business. Rhodolphus Sheldon described the July 26, 1863 shelling of his family home:

At flood tide, when the vessels swung around presenting their broadsides to the house, without a word of warning, they opened fire on it and the Carpenter House with long parrot shells. It was twelve o'clock noon; we had not eaten dinner which was on the range cooking. At the first crash of shells through the house we all fled to the woods. Two hours afterward came one of the hardest showers I ever experienced and drenched us to the skin. The boats ceased firing during the shower and I stole up to the house by the rear entrance and succeeded in packing up enough food to last us two days. They opened again while I was there and a shell came through the parlor but a few feet from me and sliced off the top of our piano as nicely as though cut with a knife. They continued shelling all night and in the morning sent a party ashore which burned all that was left of both houses.

It would not be long before the family returned and began life anew, however:

As soon as we could after the close of the war, in the fall of 1865, we came back and built a smaller house upon the same site. It was made largely of wreck timber picked up on the beach; the floor was of puncheon, hewn lank split from logs, the shingles were split out and shaved with a drawing knife on a draw horse. For some years it was the only house on the present site of New Smyrna. Ora Carpenter never came back, but settled at Osteen, some miles west. He sold his land to Edmund K. Lowd, who built there the present Ocean House, except the northern part, which was added by Captain Frank W. Sams.[44]

The Sheldon building was demolished around 1903, and the property changed hands several times. During the Great Depression, WPA workers added walls and made the ruins more "fort-like" in order to further the theory that this was a military structure. A more realistic theory is that the ruins were a building foundation, possibly one built during the Turnbull era in anticipation of a visit by Turnbull partners Sir William and Lady Mary Duncan. Another possible option is that the ruins are the foundation of a large storehouse or other industrial structure.

Both theories are possible. We know that Turnbull wrote to Duncan in the summer of 1772: "I will begin a house for you next year as a venture." Turnbull relied on his partners for continued funding. It was important to put forth the idea that all was well with the settlement, and a foundation such as this would have been able to support a grand house fitting the importance of the Duncan family. The storehouse theory could be plausible due to the proximity to the town wharf. Goods were regularly arriving and being shipped out of the settlement. It would be important for these items to have a well-protected location before leaving or before being distributed.

While it might be fun to speculate about the ruins, it is important to remember that theories are just that: theories. At this time, archaeologists and historians still seek a definitive construction date and reason for the ruins being there. While that continues, it is most important to preserve the ruins. Future archaeologists and historians will need them when more information comes to light. Future generations of children will need them to look at with wonder and develop fanciful stories. The city of New Smyrna Beach needs these ruins as a novel and interesting tourist attraction to help set the city apart from others.

WAR MEMORIAL

The centerpiece of Riverside Park is an unusual-looking monument with a cross, battle helmet and eagle on the top of a large coquina mass. While the plaques on the monument show respect to veterans and casualties of several wars, the original intent was to honor "world war heroes." The official monument name is Volusia County Memorial to World War Heroes, but it often goes by the name of Veteran's Monument or War Memorial.

Friday, November 11, 1927, Armistice Day—as our current Veterans Day was then called—was a busy day in New Smyrna. All businesses were to be closed at the urging of Mayor W.C. Chowning, and thousands of people were expected to be in the downtown area for the festivities. The day started off with a 10:00 a.m. parade that began at the corner of Orange and Canal Streets. It traveled east on Canal until reaching Hillsboro Street (the modern-day Riverside Drive), turned south on Hillsboro until reaching Lytle Avenue (the approximate location of today's South Bridge) and then turned west until reaching its end at Orange Street.

At 11:00 a.m., the park activities started with a two-minute period of silence in honor of the world war veterans who had "gone west." The invocation was then given by Reverend Dr. Frank W. Gee, chaplain of the Daytona Beach American Legion Post. Dr. Harry Walker then opened the ceremonies. The flag was raised on a new flagpole donated by W.D. Werfelman. A speech about the American Legion was given by Mr. Winesmann, the post commander from the Deland American Legion.

Principal speaker Dr. Harry Walker then gave the Armistice Day address. He asked those in attendance to remember several things. First, he asked that they remember that just nine years earlier, the greatest war ever seen had ended. Second, he asked that people remember that the root causes of the war, particularly selfishness, were still in evidence. It was important to forgive but not forget. Third, it was important to remember the thousands of dead so that future war would be prevented. His fourth reminder was that those who had perished died Christ-like deaths through their sacrifice. Lastly, those who perhaps should have died were to be remembered: "There is life worse than death—blind, armless, legs gone, suffering, sick, scattered all over the country unfitted for life. But they gave it all gladly to crush out this awful demon 'selfishness' from the world." His address included a dramatic reading of the poem "In Flanders Fields." This was followed by the dedication of the monument by Dr. Davis Forster and then the benediction by Reverend Gee. Members of the American Legion then formed a parade that marched to the local post headquarters for lunch.

The afternoon was filled with family events, including Boy Scout activities in Riverside Park, YMCA activities at the local baseball field, an exhibition by the New Smyrna and Coronado Beach Fire Departments and an afternoon high school football game that saw New Smyrna take on Titusville.

This view of the War Memorial in Riverside Park was taken prior to 1959, when a six-foot-tall bronze eagle, cross and helmet were added to the top. Originally created for World War I veterans, there are now mentions of World War II and Korean War veterans on it as well. *Courtesy of the author.*

To show just how the war had brought Americans together was the meeting and friendship developed between Civil War veterans Morrison K. Lewis, Union, and Dr. Samuel W. Carroll, who entered the Confederate army at the tender age of fourteen in 1864. Carroll was captured in early 1865 and held prisoner until April. The two men, then advanced in age, sat down to discuss their war memories, after which they declared, "We're brothers now." Lewis is buried in Edgewater–New Smyrna Cemetery, and Carroll is buried in Pinewood Cemetery in Daytona Beach.

The setting of the sun did not damper the day's activities. At 7:30 p.m., the thirty-five-piece Volusia County Military Band played for those at Riverside Park, and at 8:30 p.m., residents were treated to what was called a "grand display of fireworks." The evening closed out with a Grand Ball called "A Night in Gay Paree" at the Women's Club. The ball featured Red Dean's Orchestra.[45]

January 31, 1959, saw the War Memorial rededicated and the unveiling of a six-foot-tall bronze eagle, cross and helmet placed atop the memorial. Also dedicated was a plaque containing the names of local men who had lost their lives in service of their country. Local dignitaries on hand included Walter T. Slattery, master of ceremonies; Mayor R.L. Arnau; members of the clergy from various denominations; and members from various local veterans' organizations. Many of these organizations contributed to the cost of the bronze eagle.

The honor of unveiling the new addition to the monument was given to Sarah Elizabeth McGehee, president of the local Gold Star Mothers chapter. Mrs. McGehee's husband, Alvin, was a World War I veteran, and the McGehees had lost their son, Alvin Jr., during World War II. Alvin Jr. is buried in St. Augustine National Cemetery. Several items relating to the McGehee family service may be seen at the New Smyrna Museum of History.[46]

On Veterans Day in 1982, several local veterans' organizations and their auxiliaries donated a plaque dedicated to the veterans of both the Korean and Vietnam Wars. In attendance were representatives from the local Veterans of Foreign Wars, American Legion and the Disabled Veterans of America (DVA). The plaque was unveiled by Bill Gerhart, service officer from the DVA. Also in attendance was the family of James E. Lawman, a Vietnam veteran who had tragically taken his own life just over a week earlier.

Rick Weeks, commander of the DVA Post 53, was one of the day's speakers, and he reminded those in attendance:

> *How much did we ask of our veterans? Think about the World War I veteran who choked on mustard gas. Think about the sailor who lost an arm or a leg when his boat was torpedoed in the South Pacific in World War II. Think about the nightmares of prisoners of war. Think about the confused Vietnam veterans who suffer flashbacks sometimes with tragic results. Is it possible to do too much for those who gave so much to make the freedom we enjoy a reality? With the passing of the years, the baton to keep this day sacred in the hearts of all Americans has passed from veterans of World War I and II to the Korean veterans and now to the veterans of Vietnam. We must not forget them nor the price they paid for our freedom.*[47]

VIETNAM MEMORIAL

Located near the coquina War Memorial in Riverside Park sits the Vietnam Memorial, a small, understated reminder of the sacrifices made by our military forces, both volunteer and drafted, during the 1960s and 1970s. As did every corner of the United States, New Smyrna Beach and the surrounding areas proudly, yet reluctantly, sent their young men off to serve

On Veterans Day 1968, the local Jaycees dedicated a monument to those soldiers who paid the ultimate price during the Vietnam War. The names of the seven men on the monument serve as a lasting reminder of the sacrifice made by local families in the effort to fight Communism. *Courtesy of the author.*

in areas that many probably couldn't have found on the map and possibly could not pronounce. This monument is dedicated to those who did not return alive.

On November 11, 1968, Veterans Day, the marker was dedicated by the local Jaycees during a public ceremony attended by locals and a local fifth grade class from Faulkner Elementary school led by Mrs. Frances M. Chandler.

Master of ceremonies Chris Nicewander oversaw the event, which featured the New Smyrna Beach High School band playing before the ceremony began. For this, it received an American flag. The featured speaker was Lanier Smith, who was retired from the United States Marine Corps. Many local organizations—including the Jaycees, VFW Post 4250, World War Barracks 79, American Legion Post 17, the Cities of New Smyrna Beach and Edgewater, the Jane Sheldon Chapter of the Daughters of the American Revolution and Gold Star Mothers—all laid wreaths in honor of the soldiers. Also in attendance were three-year-old Danny Robertson and his mother. Danny's father, Corporal John C. Robertson, who entered the army in August 1959, was killed in Vietnam on March 22, 1966.[48]

In total, seven men have their names attached to this monument: John C. Robertson, Mathew D. Renfroe, Russell A. Loeffler, Kenneth Bryan Morris, William Joseph Deuerling, Joseph P. Clerkin and Walter S. Hathaway. Five are buried in Edgewater–New Smyrna Cemetery, Private Renfroe is buried in Glencoe-Geiger Cemetery and William Deuerling is buried in Arlington National Cemetery.

AHEPA MONUMENT

Located in Riverside Park to the north of the War Memorial sits a much more modern-looking monument with a bright white marble exterior topped with four stained-glass pieces and black granite walkways around and through it. This monument, called the New Smyrna Odyssey, is the work of the AHEPA and is one of both beauty and controversy.

After years of discussion regarding where it should be built, the AHEPA was allowed to build this monument in Riverside Park. The final cost of the monument was almost $300,000. The granite and marble monument, highlighted with stained-glass pieces, serves as a reminder of the struggles the original colonists encountered when they arrived here. *Courtesy of the author.*

The water tower in Old Fort Park had hardly been down a year in 1995, when the AHEPA put forth its idea to the city commission for a twelve- by twelve-foot monument that would stand twenty feet high and sit on the spot where the water tower had been for over forty years. Having received an OK from the Historic New Smyrna Beach Preservation Committee, the AHEPA stood before the commission asking for its blessing before embarking on a fundraising drive for over $200,000, which was needed to construct the monument. Little disagreement was heard that night other than Larry Sweett making sure that any text carved on the monument be historically accurate. Just a few short years later, attitudes changed.[49]

Armed with the apparent blessings of the powers that be, the AHEPA began a national fundraising drive. It created an elaborate brochure touting the achievements and permissions already obtained:

- *Project site has been unanimously approved by the New Smyrna Beach City Council and AHEPA membership.*
- *Brother Xepapas'* [Anargyros "Andy" N. Xepapas] *design has been approved by the City of New Smyrna Beach and the Historical Society.*
- *AHEPA Citrus District 2 Convention approved the project.*
- *The 1994 AHEPA National Convention approved this memorial as a national project.*
- *And…in December 1995, The New Smyrna Odyssey was approved as a 501(c)(3) non-profit entity.*

Included in the brochure was an elaborate diagram highlighting what a donor would receive for various contribution levels. For those wishing to go all in, there were three stained-glass pieces available at the top of the monument. These were available for donations of $20,000 to $25,000.[50]

While the Old Fort Park area seemed like a lock, by October 1998, the tide—and politics—had turned against the AHEPA, and the plan was being revisited. The Historic New Smyrna Beach Preservation Committee, with new members, began backtracking. Archaeologist and committee member Dr. Roger Grange was correct when he pointed out, "This is an archaeological site that has significant archaeological objects in areas. This was part of the Turnbull area. Now the City Commission wants to dig 19 holes and run trenches for the cables. This is certain to have an impact on archaeological resources. I am distressed by this." Commissioner Larry Sweett joined in, adding, "We will destroy the ambience and history of the area. I don't believe a monolith is the way to honor the Greeks who were a part of the colony."[51]

The year 1999 brought more objections from the public. In January, Southeast Volusia Historical Society president Gene Sheldon wrote to the city commissioners, mayor and city manager outlining why the society felt Old Fort Park was the wrong location for the monument. Sheldon cited four reasons, backing them with strong arguments: 1) historic significance, 2) character and ambiance, 3) Civil War battle reenactments and 4) precedence.

By March, the Parks and Recreation Board was also publicly expressing concerns, as was city commissioner Jo Ann O'Bannon. O'Bannon felt the monument to be too large and out of character with the park. The Parks and Recreation Board stated that the monument would not be in keeping with the integrity of the park. It also objected to the size and materials that would be used.[52]

It is important to note that those in opposition had not stated they were against the monument; rather, they were against placing it in Old Fort Park. Their belief was that another location could be found where the monument fit into the surroundings and would not potentially damage archaeologically rich ground.

As April drew to a close and the outside temperatures started to soar, cooler heads started to prevail. After a city commission meeting, it was mutually decided that a new location should be found. Several options were quickly tossed around, including the entrance to the city, where Highway 44 and Canal Street come together; the far-east end of Canal Street; and Riverside Park. Ultimately, eight sites were reviewed by the AHEPA, historical society representatives and city employees before a decision was reached.

By June, it was agreed that the new monument would be built in Riverside Park in an area located to the north of the War Memorial. This, however, was not the end of the disagreements. Architect Andy Xepapas was upset with the delays: "I am sick and tired of being given the run-around for the last six years by the city. The conceptual plans are based on a decision that was made six years ago." With the new location, the monument was downsized: "The monument's base is only 128 square feet now to the original 455 square feet. The height of the monument is 20 feet down from 23 feet."

In mid-July, the final details were worked out regarding the placement of the monument. It was also agreed that the AHEPA would be responsible for landscaping the area, the costs of electrical connections and all maintenance of the marble and granite monument.

After six years of discussions, arguments, accusations and more, construction was finally started in April 2000. The groundbreaking ceremony was led by Father Nick Manousakis, who stated, "This land was gained by honest sweat." Once completed, the monument cost between $250,000 and $300,000. Included with the names of sponsors was a history titled "The New Smyrna Odyssey, 1768–1777," written by T.C. Wilder, JoAnne Sikes and Gary Luther. As Ms. Sikes said about the project, "This is a wonderful credit to the community."[53]

OLD WHARF MARKER

Driving south from downtown, you will come to a small island located in Riverside Drive near Clinch Avenue. Off to the east, located between two trees, sits a small coquina marker with a bronze tablet attached. This marker actually serves a dual role, covering both the Turnbull-era wharf and a Civil War skirmish.

The actual remains of the wharf are best seen at low tide. These large blocks of stone extend approximately eighty feet into the Indian River. In the river, there is a marker calling attention to the site and making those

A coquina marker and bronze plaque mark the site of the Turnbull-era wharf. The wharf remains are best seen at low tide. The marker, placed in 1940 by the Jane Sheldon Chapter of the Daughters of the American Revolution, also marks the spot of a March 1862 Civil War skirmish. *Courtesy of the author.*

The remains of the Turnbull-era wharf can be seen extending into the Indian River just off Riverside Drive. The wharf was at the center of activity during the Turnbull years. Supplies arrived here, and crops being sent to England left from here. The ruins are viewable only at low tide and should not be disturbed. *Courtesy of the Southeast Volusia Historical Society.*

viewing the wharf remains aware that it is against the law to disturb them. The wharf area is thought to be the major hub of the Turnbull settlement, the area where supplies were received and crops loaded to be sent to Europe for sale. The wharf also marked the end point of the King's Highway.

This area is important to New Smyrna history for another reason. It was in this area that a small skirmish took place in 1862 during the Civil War. By 1862, the Union blockade was well underway, and blockade-running was a dangerous yet highly profitable activity—one also seen as vital to the Confederate war effort.

Mosquito Inlet was a prime entry point for blockade-runners. The shifting sands made it dangerous for large blockaders to enter, but the more shallow-draft blockade-runners were much more likely to have a successful run into the river. The *Henry Andrew* and the *Penguin* were assigned the area and learned of the possibility that the *Kate* (sometimes referred to as *Katie*) could be hiding in the inlet.

On March 22, a launch of six lightly armed boats containing forty-three men led by Captain Mather and Lieutenant Budd, along with a "Negro" guide, set out to find the blockade-runner and investigate the area. The boats headed south through the New Smyrna area, eventually finding the *Kate* and leaving a prize crew with it. Confederate troops led by Captain Bird and Captain Strain, both of the Third Florida Infantry, were in the area guarding a supply of arms and ammunition. The Confederates took note of the southbound troops and set up near the wharf area to await their return.

After the successful trip, and having no fear of Confederate troops in the area, the Union boats dropped their guard during the return trip. When the lead boat came too near shore, Captain Strain began firing on the crew. Both Captain Mather and Lieutenant Budd were killed, along with six crew members. Six more were wounded, and two were taken prisoner, including the black guide. The crews of the other two boats were more fortunate and took shelter on the other side of the river; their crews forged their way back to the inlet to meet with the *Henry Andrew*.

On the morning of March 23, Union troops returned under a flag of truce. They were met by Captain Bird, who returned the bodies of the two officers and their possessions. The black guide had been taken inland and hanged.

Thus ended the first Civil War skirmish in New Smyrna. The blockade continued, and Mosquito Inlet continued to be an entry and exit point for blockade-runners. While there was further military activity in the area in 1863, there is no evidence supporting that the Sheldon Hotel was destroyed in a retaliation bombing, as is often suggested.[54]

5
Coronado Beach (As It Used to Be Known)

It was the struggle of a small community trying to live.
—James G. Schauwecker, former mayor of Coronado Beach

The area now known as beachside New Smyrna Beach used to be a completely separate city known as Coronado Beach. Coronado Beach was originally the name for land owned by Foster G. Austin. This area lay approximately one mile south of today's Flagler Avenue. The area is often referred to as "Old Coronado." According to historian Gary Luther, it is possible that the name Coronado could have come from the Southern California city with the same name.

Until the first bridge was built in 1892, the best way to cross the Indian River was by ferry or boat. The 1892 bridge did not last long, however, and was quickly destroyed by a hurricane. By March 1894, relief was available in the form of a toll bridge. The new bridge was built and managed by the New Smyrna Bridge and Investment Company, led by Washington E. Connor. The company was originally formed with $15,000 of investment capital and quickly began producing a return for the investors.

Always the businessman, Connor knew this revenue stream would not last forever. By the early 1920s, the bridge was in need of costly repairs, and a competing "south" bridge was on the verge of becoming a reality. Connor hatched a plan to rid himself of the bridge but still look to be a good citizen. He offered to donate the Connor Library (now the CRA building in Old Fort Park) to the city if the county would purchase his bridge. In 1925,

This early 1940s postcard view of the bridge that led to Coronado Beach might lead those viewing it to think there was nothing beachside. However, waiting on the other side of the bridge were businesses such as the Riverview Hotel and the Casino, where beachgoers could have a meal, enjoy a drink and listen to live music. *Courtesy of the author.*

the state approved $32,500 for the county to purchase the bridge, and New Smyrna was given the library.[55]

A long told yet incorrect myth says that New Smyrna changed its name to New Smyrna Beach when Coronado Beach was annexed into the city. Rather, these events happened nearly a decade apart and have no relation to each other. Beach was added to New Smyrna officially by the United States Post Office on August 1, 1937. New Smyrna voters had approved this change earlier in the year. When asked about the change, local postmaster William Playters Wilkinson said that "to continue the harmonious conduct of business, and as local people seemingly were accepting the change without protest, it would be advisable to accept the change." In an article in the local paper, stamp collectors were reminded that if they wanted last New Smyrna and first New Smyrna Beach cancellations, they had to have their envelopes at the post office on July 31, 1937. About 250 letters were sent, each bearing the historic postmarks. It was also reported that many asked Postmaster Wilkinson to sign their souvenirs.[56]

Nearly a decade later, as the voting day for city consolidation came closer, the *News* ran frequent updates and reminders that

Millard Caldwell served as the twenty-ninth governor of Florida from 1945 to 1949. He had the distinction of serving in all three branches of government: as Florida governor, as U.S. representative from Florida and as a Florida Supreme Court justice. *Courtesy of the State Archives of Florida.*

potential voters needed to make sure they were registered. Almost eight years after New Smyrna changed its name, on May 15, 1945, the issue of Coronado Beach and New Smyrna Beach consolidating into one city came to a head when voters for both municipalities approved the merger. The measure passed in Coronado Beach by 29 votes and in New Smyrna Beach by 357 votes. This referendum election was made possible after the state senate and House of Representatives passed a bill that was signed into law by then governor Millard Caldwell allowing the two cities to determine whether they would become one.

On Monday, April 1, 1946, the city of Coronado Beach was officially merged into the city of New Smyrna Beach. The new city commission consisted of members J.A. Sapp, H.K. Pierson, E.E. Altman, Lot Atkinson and O.M. Poole. Even before the official consolidation, the issue of water on the beachside was being discussed. "City manager J.C. Ferris suggested the extension of water lines to the beach side as one of the main projects. He said the present water system, including the softening plant, is operating satisfactorily but will soon be inadequate to serve the growing population." As former Coronado Beach mayor James G. Schauwecker said in a 1974 interview, "Water and electric for Coronado came from New Smyrna. Actually, we gave the town away to get New Smyrna water over here."[57]

The 2015 creation of the Coronado Island Neighborhood is just a recycling of the name Coronado. The area that is included in this neighborhood is what is traditionally called the North Causeway. Based on city maps, the newly named area extends from the east side of Riverside Drive until halfway across the north bridge. This land was never considered part of Coronado Beach, and the name was brought into existence in order to help market the area for redevelopment.

CHARLES DUMMETT GRAVE SITE

One of the oddest sites in New Smyrna Beach is a single-stone cemetery located in a residential area just over the North Causeway Bridge in the middle of Canova Drive. The timeworn and cracked vault provides us with information on who is buried there but not why.

The inscription on the marker reads, "Sacred to the Memory of Charles Dummett Born August 18, 1844–Died April 23, 1860." But who was Charles Dummett (or Dummitt, as his name is sometimes spelled)? How did he come to be buried in the middle of a road in a residential area? How did Canova Drive get its name?

Young Charles was the son of Douglas Dummett. Originally from Barbados, Douglas made the most of an inheritance from his father, Thomas, and became a man of some wealth and fame. The Dummett

Now a popular bed-and-breakfast, the St. Francis Inn, located in St. Augustine, was purchased by Thomas Dummett in 1838. Thomas's son, Douglas, later lived at Coronado Beach. Douglas's son, Charles, was killed in a hunting accident, and it is said that Douglas buried Charles where he died. His tomb is located in the middle of Canova Drive in a residential area. *Courtesy of the State Archives of Florida.*

family immigrated to the United States in the late 1790s after the Slave Trade Act abolished slavery in all British territories. They settled in Connecticut, where Douglas attended Yale University. The family later moved to Florida, taking up residence in St. Augustine, where they lived in what is now the St. Francis Inn bed-and-breakfast. This building is sometimes inaccurately called the "Governor's Palace." Douglas had sisters who achieved a certain level of fame themselves. Elizabeth married a gentleman by the name of William Hardee. After a solid career in the United States Army, Hardee served as a general in the Confederate army and is also known for his book, often referred to as *Hardee's Tactics*. Another of Douglas's sisters, Anna, was often considered to be a Confederate spy by the Union forces occupying St. Augustine.

During the Second Seminole War, Douglas served as a captain in Company B of the Second Regiment, Second Brigade, of the Florida militia. This regiment often went by the nickname "Mosquito Roarers." Douglas was severely wounded in the neck and did not return to service. His bravery, however, was never questioned, and James Ormond III wrote about him: "There was one man in the fight that I do not think ever knew what fear was—that was our Captain Douglas Dummett."

After the war and a failed marriage, Douglas moved to the area that would be known as Coronado Beach. It is said that Douglas took a slave by the name of Anna to be his wife, and it was accepted knowledge that they had three daughters and a son. In his will, Douglas referenced his three surviving daughters, who had a mother by the name of Leandra, a name that could easily have been shortened to Anna.

Charles was born in a still wild area of Florida on August 18, 1844. He appears to have had a normal upbringing until being sent north in order to receive a "proper education." In April 1860, as the clouds of approaching war grew darker, Charles was home from school. What happened next has been a mystery for over 150 years. There are wild theories and then what is the widely accepted story.

The first theory is that young Charles was killed accidentally by a hunting partner. Another theory is that Charles committed suicide, ostensibly due to having taken abuse while at school due to his being of mixed race. While there is no credible evidence to prove or disprove either of these ideas, neither is seen as the probable reason for Charles's death.

What is more likely to have happened was a hunting accident. Charles was hunting in the then densely grown area between the Atlantic Ocean and the Hillsborough River. It is likely that Charles tripped or was caught

Located in the middle of a residential area on Canova Drive is the solitary grave of Charles Dummett. It is believed Dummett was killed in a hunting accident, and his grieving father buried the young man where he died. Canova Drive is named for the late actress Judy Canova. *Courtesy of the Southeast Volusia Historical Society.*

up in brush and his gun discharged, the bullet striking him and killing him instantly.

Douglas, a devastated father, buried his only son where he fell. When he later sold his real estate holdings in New Smyrna, he stipulated in the deed that the grave of his son could not be moved. More than 150 years later, the now heavily worn and broken tomb still sits in the middle of a road in a residential area.

The fact that it is still there does not mean there have not been attempts to have it removed. In 1949, radio, film and television actress Judy Canova suggested developing the area into a trailer park. This was denied by the city, and she later had the land platted as the H.L. Canova Subdivision. The road that Charles's grave divides is now called Canova Drive.

In 1953, city commissioner Hannah Bonnet asked if it would be possible to have the grave moved to the Coronado Cemetery (I believe she was referring to what is commonly called the Detwiler Cemetery today). City attorney C. Winston Smith stated the belief that "it would be extremely difficult to locate all of the heirs of the boy in order to obtain

Judy Canova was a star in radio, television and movies. She also saw the value of developing beachside land in New Smyrna Beach. Even though her ultimate goal was not achieved, Canova Drive is named for her. *Courtesy of the Library of Congress.*

permission to move the body and that the courts lean over backwards to preserve a grave." It appears nothing further came of her request, and the grave still sits on Canova Drive.

In recent years, many locals have taken it upon themselves to care for the crumbling monument to a young boy. In April 2012, the New Smyrna Beach City Commission unanimously passed a resolution designating the grave a local historic landmark.[58]

WATCH AND WARN AIRCRAFT WARNING SERVICE MONUMENT

During World War II, the entire United States coastline was on high alert, whether it be for German submarines or planes or an attack from the Japanese. Being ever patriotic, the citizens of New Smyrna came to the service of their country in an effort to help protect against any enemy attack.

The Watch and Warn AWS Monument is unique in that it was placed during the time those it is commemorating were active. During the years 1942–44, local volunteers would climb to a platform on the beachside water tower in order to watch for enemy planes. These towers were set up all along the coast and served as a "radar" system, allowing the army to keep track of aircraft. *Courtesy of the author.*

These volunteers—both men and women, young and old—are commemorated by an old stone monument located on Columbus Avenue near the corner of Pine Street. This is commonly called the Watch and Warn AWS Monument. (AWS stands for Aircraft Warning Service.)

Prior to its demolition in March 1973, there was a water tower located beachside. From May 29, 1942, until May 29, 1944, there was a platform built below the tower allowing the dedicated volunteer group clear views of the sky in order to watch for enemy aircraft. Volunteers were given a few days' training and had to pass an aircraft identification test before being allowed to climb the steel steps in service to their country. Once there, they did have reference materials to help them identify various types of aircraft. Volunteers worked two- to four-hour shifts, and the tower was manned twenty-four hours per day. When a plane was spotted—which, according to Russell Smith, happened perhaps once per hour—the volunteer would have to call it in to military authorities in either Orlando or Jacksonville. They would provide as much information as possible, including the direction and number of engines. There do not appear to be any records of enemy aircraft being spotted in the New Smyrna area.

One thing that makes this monument unique is that it was originally dedicated less than six months after the AWS started service in New Smyrna. The second unique aspect of the monument is that it serves a dual role. Not only does it commemorate the AWS, but it also serves as a monument to the Surruque Indians, who are said to have built the first lookout post in the area.

The monument itself is rather simple. Below the date of May 1942 is the U.S. Army Air Force logo. The text below that reads, "Coronado Beach Watch and Warn No Plane—Be It Friendly or Foe Must Pass Unchallenged A.W.S. Observers." Surrounding the monument are pavers containing the names of 132 individuals who served as watchers. Many of these names are no longer readable and are lost to time. In 1999, with the help of Marion Riensema, a near complete list of names was created.

While honoring those who were watching for enemies in 1942, the monument builders paid homage to those who came before with the same goal. According to a large stone placed in front of the monument, the Surruque Indians had built a lookout post in the area as early as 1342. The stone reads:

The Legend
600 Years ago, this was
the land of the Surocs [sic].
Their village was at
Turtle Mound, eight mi.
south of this tower.
A hurricane had laid
low the dunes used as
their lookouts. Scouts
reported that Indians
from the north country
were on the war path
—The chief speaks—
"Suroc nation must have
dune for lookout—Old
dune gone—make new—
of shells—make high—
as mountain—see far—
see enemy—kill—"

The October 18, 1942 dedication of the monument and tower was a major event for the small town of Coronado Beach. According to the *New Smyrna Beach News*, "Hundreds of persons attended the program at which the Coronado Beach observation post of the Aircraft Warning Service and a memorial to Turtle Mound which is believed to be the first lookout built in the United States, were dedicated." Some of the local dignitaries attending the afternoon event included W.J. Finn, the East Volusia County director of the AWS; New Smyrna Beach mayor W.E. Swoope; Coronado Beach mayor O.E. Taylor; and chief observer Glenn D. Evy, along with his three principal assistants. Chief observers from the Oak Hill, Port Orange and Glencoe AWS posts were also in attendance. J.U. Gillespie, the New Smyrna Beach city attorney, gave the main address, which outlined a mythological story of the building of Turtle Mound. Members of the U.S. Army and U.S. Coast Guard were on hand, and the New Smyrna Beach High School band, led by Mrs. U.J. Burrows, played patriotic songs at the start and conclusion of the event. The opening invocation was given by the Reverend Eldred C. Simpkins, vicar of St. Paul's Episcopal Church, and the closing benediction was provided by the Reverend C.H. Summers from Coronado Beach Community Methodist Church. After the event, Mr. Finn invited those in attendance to visit the post located at the Coronado Beach water tower.

On March 2, 1973, the water tower that had given service during World War II was dismantled. The ravages weathered by being so close to the ocean had finally taken their toll, and with the improvements in technology, a water tower was no longer needed.

On the fifty-seventh anniversary of the opening of the Coronado Beach AWS in 1999, the Men's Garden Club of New Smyrna Beach held a rededication ceremony of the monument. The club had cleaned the area and put in new landscaping. During the ceremony, New Smyrna Beach mayor James Vandergrifft commented, "I am proud to be here to honor those who served to protect us. I am not old enough to remember this, but we should honor those who gave of themselves to perform this duty." Surviving watchers or their descendants who were in attendance were invited to introduce themselves. Men's Garden Club president Bill Brown then remarked, "I hope all of you will take the time once in a while to stop by and look at this monument. Bring your children and tell them about the people that served to protect us during a time of war. We salute all of the watchers for their fine work." Mr. Brown's words still ring true today.[59]

Canaveral National Seashore

Located at the far southern end of the beachside is the northern end of Canaveral National Seashore. Cape Canaveral to the south has served as a missile-testing site since the 1950s and has been the primary launch site for NASA and other organizations sending objects into space. Out of the tens of thousands of acres owned by the government, a portion was set aside as a wildlife refuge in 1964. Canaveral National Seashore was officially founded in 1975.[60]

For our purposes, we will be only briefly discussing a few of the areas that can be found in the National Seashore located near New Smyrna Beach. A full coverage would be impossible in a book like this. For further information, it is recommended that visitors stop at the information centers provided by the National Park Service. Here you can find maps, brochures and displays and watch videos that will help orient and educate you.

Perhaps the most widely known feature of the Seashore is Turtle Mound. Turtle Mound has traditionally been associated with the Surruque Indian tribe. The mound is shown on many historical maps, and it can safely be assumed that it was used as a navigational marker by ship's captains. Turtle Mound is approximately thirty to thirty-five feet high. It is composed mostly of oyster shells and other refuse from early peoples of the area. A full archaeological excavation of the mound has not taken place, and it appears there are no plans for such an endeavor. Today, the mound is covered by dense vegetation. There have been several botanical surveys of the area done dating back to one in 1788 by Andre Michaux. The historical and archaeological value of Turtle Mound is tremendous, and as such, visitors are not allowed to directly walk on or climb it. There is a man-made walkway that will take you to the top. The views are amazing, but as with almost all of the Seashore area, it is recommended you bring your bug spray!

Turtle Mound is also unique in having survived. Similar-type mounds used to dot the coastline. These mounds, however, were destroyed in the early twentieth century, and the shells were used for roadbeds and also by railroad companies for track beds as they expanded southward.

While a full discussion of the town of Eldora is beyond the scope of this project, a brief history is certainly in order here. The area that was to become the town of Eldora was formerly occupied by native peoples and the occasional hunter. According to a National Park Service brochure, the town went through four distinct periods beginning in 1877. From 1877 through 1898, the area was primarily an agricultural community. It was also used as

Turtle Mound is located within the Canaveral National Seashore. This is not a burial mound; rather, it is considered to be waste remains and mostly consists of oyster shells. The mound sits approximately thirty feet high, and there is a man-made wooden trail that can be followed to the top. Climbing directly on the mound is forbidden. *Courtesy of the Southeast Volusia Historical Society.*

a steamboat stop before railroads ventured that far south. During this time frame, the United States Coast Guard built a "house of refuge" here (see Chapter 7, "Memories," for more information). The house of refuge was located in the area of modern-day parking lot number five. Early residents of the area came from Alabama, Georgia, Mississippi, Missouri, New York, New Jersey, England and Germany. This group of people, with wide and diverse backgrounds, brought many different skill sets and, by working together, established the bones of what was to become Eldora.

The name Eldora came from the George Pitzer family, one of the earliest pioneer families to the area. Eldora was derived from combining the names of Pitzer's daughters—Ellen and Dora. George and Cora Pitzer are buried in Edgewater–New Smyrna Cemetery, along with their son, Lee, who died of pneumonia and influenza while serving in the United States Army during the later stages of World War I. He was only eighteen years old.

As the railroad industry continued to grow, the way people traveled changed, and this affected Eldora. During the era of 1898 through 1938, the town became known more for rest, relaxation and recreation than for hard farm labor. At the turn of the century, there were fewer than two hundred residents, many of whom did not stay to witness the changes that were coming.

The change to a more tourist-based economy did not come easily, however. As the reality of the railroad approached, some residents adapted, and others moved on. The railroad lessened the need for shallow-draft boats both in terms of transportation and for shipping. Several freezes killed citrus crops and pushed growers farther south. For those who stayed, however, opportunity was knocking. The comparatively warm winters brought wealthy part-time residents to the area. Eldora earned a reputation as being a good place for hunters and fishermen. Many residents were able to make a living by providing services to the winter visitors.

The period from 1938 through 1975 proved a difficult one for Eldora. According to the NPS, there were fewer than a dozen permanent residents as the World War II era began. The Depression slammed the brakes on touring for many Americans, and the coming of war led many people to migrate to cities in search of work. Young men would soon enlist or be drafted. In the postwar years, travel continued to change rapidly. The rise of automobile ownership put more people on the roads. With the federal interstate system reaching into Florida, no longer could areas like Eldora compete with roadside attractions and the advent of massive theme parks. By 1975, it is estimated that there were fewer than five year-round residents.

The period of 1975 through the present has been positive, however, with the formation of the Canaveral National Seashore. The National Park Service now controls the land that was Eldora, thus ensuring that it will be maintained and preserved rather than fall prey to condominiums or other development.[61]

When one thinks of Eldora today, what is most likely to come to mind is a white two-story building commonly referred to as the Eldora State House. The house also goes by the name Moulton-Wells House in honor of prior owners Marion Moulton, widow of Julius Moulton, and Walter M. Wells.

The house was constructed around the years 1913 through 1926. It first appeared on county tax rolls in 1920. Mrs. Moulton passed away in 1926 and is buried in Bellefontaine Cemetery in St. Louis, Missouri. Marion's heirs sold the property to Walter M. Wells in 1927. Wells continued to work

The stately white house that serves as home to many of the exhibits dealing with Eldora and the house of refuge is commonly called the Eldora State House. It also goes by the more formal name of the Moulton-Wells House. The home dates to approximately 1913–26 and is named for prior owners Marion Moulton and Walter M. Wells. *Courtesy of the author.*

on the property by improving the landscaping, maintaining the outbuildings and creating a large garden area.

Wells was known for entertaining, and the Frank Sams family were known to be frequent visitors. It was this association that many claim led to the nickname Eldora State House. Wells passed away at his home in 1938 and is buried in Springwood Cemetery in Greenville, South Carolina. After Walter Wells's death, the Wells family continued to use the home as a winter residence for many more years before selling it in 1965.

With the National Park Service operating Canaveral National Seashore, the Eldora State House continued to sit empty and deteriorate. By 1989, a group of concerned citizens had banded together, and Friends of Canaveral was formed. Their stated goal was to preserve the Eldora State House and open it to park visitors with an emphasis on showing and interpreting the history of Eldora. Sid Corhern was elected as the first president once the group officially incorporated. After ten long years of fundraising and rehabilitation work, the Eldora State House was opened to visitors in May 1999. In November 2001, the Friends of Canaveral work fully paid off when the Eldora State House was added to the National Register of Historic

Places. It continues to be open to the public and has a nice display of photos and information about Eldora. The Eldora State House is not open all hours the park is open, so it is advisable to call ahead and verify hours before making a special trip.

As for Friends of Canaveral, the group is still active and supports the National Park Service in its mission to preserve, protect and interpret the fifty-seven thousand acres of pristine shoreline, dunes and wilderness that are Canaveral National Seashore. While they may no longer be actively preserving high-profile buildings, their influence in environmental initiatives is felt. In addition to their work protecting the natural dunes of the area, they are involved in finding and protecting endangered sea turtle nests.[62]

6

Ponce Inlet

When it came night, the white waves paced to and fro in the moonlight, and the wind brought the sound of the great sea's voice to the men on shore, and they felt that they could then be interpreters.
—Stephen Crane, The Open Boat

It is very easy to argue that the simplest and fastest way to get to Ponce Inlet from New Smyrna Beach is by boat. From the north end of New Smyrna Beach, it is only a short boat ride to the small city across the inlet. To make the same trip by car can easily take forty-five minutes or possibly longer if one hits bad traffic. Despite being small and difficult to get into and out of—there are two two-lane options, both of which can easily become congested—this is a city with much charm and is well worth the trip.

Hasty Cottage and Cemetery

Located on quiet Beach Street sits a small, remodeled, Cracker-style home, and across the street is a white-fenced cemetery. Both are reminders of the Hasty family, a family of early pioneers in the area. Nathaniel Hasty and his wife, Elizabeth, who were both transplants from Maine, built the house in 1920. The family ran a small trading post, fishing cottage and the local post office out of the small dwelling.

The Meyer-Davis House, located in Ponce Inlet, is a prime example of Cracker-style architecture. This duplex was built in the 1920s. In 1941, it became home to the Edward Meyer family. Meyer served as the last civilian lighthouse keeper in Ponce Inlet. The Meyer-Davis House, along with the Hasty Cottage next door, both of which have been fully restored, serves as home to the Ponce Inlet Historical Museum. *Courtesy of the author.*

After years of deterioration, the City of Ponce Inlet decided to have the Hasty Cottage and the Meyer-Davis House, which sits adjacent, restored. It hired architect Sidney Cohern and the Durable Restoration Company. This group used historic photos and began the long restoration process. Once complete, the city was awarded an Outstanding Achievement Award for Restoration/Rehabilitation from the Florida Trust for Historic Preservation. The two buildings now house displays and artifacts related to the city of Ponce Inlet. A volunteer guide is available who can answer questions about the museum and area in general.

Located across the street from the small buildings is the four-person cemetery that often goes by the name Hasty Cemetery. Buried in the cemetery are Nathaniel and Elizabeth Hasty. Also buried there are the infant Rebecca Hunt, who lived just over two months, and a beloved handyman by the name of Bill Williams, who was known as "Cocoa." While some stories state that Cocoa was buried in the family plot after an accident at the insistence of Nathaniel and Elizabeth, the death date on his marker, 1932, is considerably after the deaths of Nathaniel in 1907 and Elizabeth in 1909.[63]

PACETTI CEMETERY

Located on Sailfish Drive, on what appears to be a dune that is above the roadbed, sits Pacetti Cemetery. This small, overgrown family cemetery could really be located anywhere and many times would be overlooked. This cemetery, though behind a locked gate and generally not accessible, should not be pushed aside as just another small family cemetery.

While there are only nine marked graves and a dedication marker, the family buried here played an important role in the history of Mosquito Inlet. The dedication marker reads: "Pacetti Descendants of Pons Dedicated to the First Settlers of Mosquito Inlet." The patriarch and matriarch of the cemetery, so to speak, are Bartola C. Pacetti (1813 [or 1822]–1898) and Martha J. Pacetti (1846–1917). The remaining seven burials are descendants of the Pacettis.

The Pacetti story really begins with the history of how Antonio Pons, perhaps an uncle to Bartola, acquired the land that Bartola and family were to live on. In a letter dated September 26, 1803 (and written by Jose de Zabalias), Pons outlines a history of his ownership in an attempt to regain possession from a man named Hall (more likely than not Ambrose Hull, who had obtained several large Spanish land grants in the prior years):

> *That by the concessions made to me by the Governors of this province, according to the gratiousness* [sic] *that sovereign piety has bestowed upon its residents, I possess a portion of land in the ruined settlement of Mosquitos, of which I took possession early in the year 1791, going there with my entire family. Immediately upon my arrival I constructed upon it a masonry house that still exists except for the roof that was burned by the Indians. In the three years that I cultivated it, it had begun to develop as I had planned. However since in the last year it suffered incursions by Indians, who destroyed all of the crops and threatened my life and that of my family, it was necessary for me to return to this city in order to protect what was dear to me…*
>
> *Several days ago Hall* [sic] *appeared requesting the same lands that Dupont had told him were mine, and being known to him all of the aforesaid regarding them, his request is malicious and his intention so bad as that of wishing to destroy and ruin an old and poor settler who must provide for his family by the strength of his arms, the pious intentions of Sovereign being equal for all, rich or poor.*

Pons's appeal for justice succeeded, and Spanish land grants show "175 acres at the mouth of Halifax River south of St. Augustine, bounded on the north by vacant land, south by district known as Mosquitoes or New Smyrna east by the ocean west by the river; granted 10/11/1803."

Bartola Pacetti arrived in the area in 1843. He worked as a harbor pilot, helping navigate boats through the inlet that were taking live oak timbers north to be used in the shipbuilding industry. His brother, Gomezinda (sometimes seen spelled Gomecindo), also lived in the area. Around 1858, the heirs of Antonio Pons deeded the 175-acre grant to the Pacetti brothers.

In 1860, Bartola married the then fourteen-year-old Martha Jane Wickwire. Shortly after their marriage, the Civil War broke out. It appears that Bartola served for a short time in the Eighth Florida, Company D. According to Harman and Coles, Bartola enlisted in November 1861 and deserted in October 1864, taking the oath of allegiance later that month in City Point, Virginia. He was provided transport home. There is no record that he or his wife received a pension from the state. It is important to note that two different Bartola Pacettis served in the Florida infantry during the Civil War. The other, Bartola J. Pacetti, served as a member of the Third Florida, Company B.

During the last of the war years, it appears the newlyweds lived a bit more inland, possibly in the Spruce Creek area. After the war, Gomezinda and his wife returned to Cuba, leaving Bartola and Martha as owners of the Ponce Park property. Bartola returned to find his home badly damaged. Despite this, they continued to reside in the area.

It was widely known that the inlet was very dangerous. The federal government had put off building a lighthouse until 1882 and 1883, when $30,000 was appropriated each year. The lighthouse was to be both positive and tragic for the Pacetti family. In 1883, they agreed to sell ten acres to the United States government for use as grounds for the lighthouse. The Pacettis received $400 when the title was cleared in 1884. Funding continued, though at a slow pace, and work went on through 1887. During the 1886 work, Bartola and Martha's son Henry was working aboard a barge that was bringing a load of bricks to shore. While attempting to help dock the barge, Henry's leg was caught in the thick rope being used to moor the boat and ripped from his body. Shockingly, Henry did not immediately die from his injuries but instead lived until December 1888. Tragically, on the same day as Henry's injury, his young wife, Lula, passed away during childbirth.

During the 1880s, the Pacettis were befriended by a young man by the name of William Aiken Walker. Today, Walker is a well-known painter, mostly associated with southern scenes. Walker convinced the Pacettis of the need for a boardinghouse for the many northerners who were discovering the fishing and hunting pleasures of the area. In 1886, the Pacetti Boardinghouse was completed. This became the family business, with both children and grandchildren helping operate it. Walker was hired on as the office keeper and registrar, a job he would hold for more than twenty years. For his labors, Walker received room and board. He found the area most conducive to his painting and would on occasion give one of his works to the Pacetti family. More often, however, he would be able to sell his paintings to the guests. They took them home as a reminder of their Florida trip.

Bartola C. Pacetti passed away in 1898. The family decided he should be buried in the Catholic cemetery located in his hometown of St. Augustine. His sons dutifully took the body north only to be told by the priest that he would not allow the burial because Bartola was a freemason (Bartola is recorded as serving as junior warden for Halifax Lodge No. 81 in 1877). It was imperative to find a burial location for the body, so the casket was filled with port wine (presumably as an embalming technique) and returned to Ponce Park. Here, Bartola was laid to rest outside the back gate of his property.

Buried alongside Bartola are his wife, Martha; daughter, Saraphina; and Saraphina's husband, Captain John Gardner. Also in the cemetery are John and Saraphina's sons William G. and John L., along with John's wife, Isabel, and daughter, Martha Elinor Gardner Gore, and Math Douglas Wilson, a U.S. Marine Corps veteran from World War II and husband of Eva Gardner, John and Saraphina's daughter. Eva appears to have been Math's third wife; he was previously married to Myrtle, whom he divorced in 1935, and Ester Mae Teston, who passed away in 1966. Math and Eva Gardner Dagley married in July 1967.[64]

PONCE INLET LIGHTHOUSE

The inlet we now call Ponce Inlet was originally known by the less flattering name of Mosquito Inlet. It received this moniker in 1569 from Captain Antonio de Prado because of the large number of small and annoying insects.

As the spoils of war shifted, Great Britain would ultimately come to rule Florida in 1763 as part of the Treaty of Paris after the French and Indian War (the Seven Years' War). Great Britain divided the territory into West and East Florida. East Florida had St. Augustine as its capital, while

Patrick Tonyn served as the second colonial governor of East Florida during the years 1774–83. It was Tonyn who freed the indentured servants of Andrew Turnbull in 1777. Many of those freed were of Minorcan descent and settled in St. Augustine. *Courtesy of the State Archives of Florida.*

Pensacola served as the capital of West Florida. During the sixteen years of British rule, East Florida would have five governors. It was during the British period that the need for a light of some kind at the often-dangerous inlet was first met. Governor Patrick Tonyn established a "beacon" that would help ship's captains navigate the often-shifting sandbar. Author Thomas W. Taylor speculates that the beacon "was probably nothing more than a large fire lit and kept burning on a high sand dune."

Florida was to continue changing hands based on the outcome of wars that were not fought on its soil. Florida was returned to Spain after the American Revolution, and then in the 1821 Adams-Onis Treaty, the United States acquired the Florida territory in exchange for assuming approximately $5,000,000 in claims against Spain. Florida would not become an official state until 1845.

Realizing the dangerous nature of the inlet, the United States Congress appropriated $11,000 for the construction of a lighthouse at Mosquito Inlet during June 1834. Little time was wasted, and on October 31 the contract was awarded to Winslow Lewis (1770–1850). Lewis was a builder of some reputation during the early nineteenth century. He had a reputation of working quickly and cheaply. For many years, this would come back to haunt Congress.

The Mosquito Inlet lighthouse was to be located on the south side of the inlet on a high dune. The structure was to be forty-five feet tall, round and constructed of hard brick. The base was to be twenty-two feet in diameter and taper to ten and a half feet at the top. The base walls were to be three and a half feet thick, tapering to two feet thick at the top. The light itself was to consist of eleven lamps, which were designed by Lewis based on the English Argand lamp. In addition to the tower, a thirty-four- by twenty-foot keeper's quarters was to be built as well. In what seemed like record time, the contract was completed in February 1835 at a cost of just under $7,500.

After completion, it was found that the government had neglected to order oil to power the lamps. William H. Williams, who had been appointed keeper, was never able to light the tower. Still waiting for oil in October, a violent storm hit the area, and much of the dune was washed away, thus undermining the foundations of the tower. Understanding the danger, Williams managed to safely remove and store the lamps in anticipation of the damage being repaired and oil being delivered. During the Christmas 1835 Seminole Indian attacks under Coacoochee, the lighthouse was not spared. The property was ransacked, and three weeks later, during the Battle of Dunlawton, members of the Florida militia claim to have seen Coacoochee wearing a lamp reflector as part of his headdress. No repairs were ever made to the lighthouse, and in April 1836, the remains of the structure toppled into the inlet.[65]

During the Civil War years, the inlet was without a light. This helped pro-Confederate blockade-runners slip in and out of the inlet. They would deliver needed supplies that might include food and medicine but also guns and

Coacoochee, also known as Wild Cat, was a leader in the Seminole tribe during the Second Seminole War. He took part in the Christmas 1835 sacking of New Smyrna, which included ransacking the original Mosquito Inlet lighthouse. It was reported that Coacoochee was seen wearing one of the reflectors from the lighthouse during the Battle of Dunlawton several weeks later. *Courtesy of the State Archives of Florida.*

ammunition that would be carted to the St. Johns River and shipped downriver (the St. Johns flows south to north) and ultimately to the Confederate army. On several occasions during the war, Union blockade ships sent shallow-draft boats through the inlet to search out blockade-runners. This was met with mixed results. Would a light at the inlet have helped the Union blockade? That would be pure conjecture, which can be argued either way.

For over forty years, the inlet stood without a lighthouse. During these years, there continued to be reports of ships running aground. As large commercial ships continued to run aground, the clamor for a light grew louder. By 1873, the United States Lighthouse Board had scouted the area and put forth that even though there was little commercial activity going through the inlet, a light was needed between St. Augustine and Cape Canaveral. In the board's opinion, Mosquito Inlet was the most appropriate place. Its recommendation was that Congress appropriate $60,000 for the construction of a 150-foot-tall lighthouse. Congress did not act on the recommendation.

Time continued to pass, and in 1882, the board again recommended that a light be placed at Mosquito Inlet. The anticipated cost was $200,000. Congress made a small action and appropriated $30,000 for study and plans and a second $30,000 appropriation in 1883 in order to make a site selection and begin construction.

The board put forth requirements for the new structure in order to ensure long-term stability. The foundation was to be 12 feet deep in a 45-foot brick circle. The tower was to be 32 feet in diameter at the base and taper to 15 feet at the top. It was to be built to a height of 175 feet, which would be the second highest on the East Coast, behind only the light at Cape Hatteras. Ponce Inlet Lighthouse was to contain a fifteen-thousand-candlepower beam and would be visible to a distance of eighteen nautical miles by a person standing on the deck of a 15-foot-tall vessel. As technology advanced, the "light" portion of the lighthouse evolved as well.[66]

It is often repeated that Francis Hopkinson Smith, the painter, author and engineer who designed the base for the Statue of Liberty, worked as the designer for the Ponce Inlet Lighthouse. In an extensive article published by the Ponce Inlet Lighthouse Preservation Association, this myth is questioned. Francis Smith did help design other lighthouses and was often associated with Orville Babcock, who was serving as chief engineer for the United States Lighthouse Service and was supervising the Ponce Inlet construction until his death, thus leading to the confusion. Another possible reason for the confusion was the fact that Francis Smith was the builder of the ten houses of refuge located in Florida. The "Smith" who is definitively associated with the construction of the lighthouse was Jared Smith. Jared took over Babcock's role after his untimely death.[67]

Orville Babcock was born in 1835 in Franklin, Vermont, near the Canadian border. In 1861, he graduated from West Point Military Academy, third in his

Orville Babcock graduated third in his class from the United States Military Academy and was promoted to the rank of brevet brigadier general during the Civil War. Babcock was a close associate of Ulysses S. Grant and was later appointed superintendent of public buildings and inspector of lighthouses. While serving as chief engineer on the Mosquito Lagoon lighthouse project, he drowned when his boat capsized attempting to cross through the dangerous inlet. *Courtesy of the Library of Congress.*

class, and entered service in the United States Army. Babcock rose from the rank of second lieutenant to brevet brigadier general, eventually serving as aide-de-camp to Ulysses S. Grant. Babcock delivered surrender terms to Robert E. Lee and personally escorted the Confederate leader to the McLean House in Appomattox Court House, Virginia, where he witnessed the signing of the surrender documents, thus effectively ending the Civil War.

In the postwar years, Babcock continued his allegiance to Grant and served as a personal secretary. He followed Grant to Washington, D.C., after the general's election as president and served as superintendent of buildings and grounds in the city. He later became chief engineer for the Sixth District Light House Establishment, which would oversee the construction at Mosquito Inlet. On June 2, 1884, during a visit to the site, Babcock's boat overturned in the dangerous inlet. He and several others drowned while trying to build a lighthouse that might have helped prevent such tragedies. Babcock is buried in Arlington National Cemetery under a standard-issue military headstone.

In 1883 and 1884, the land for the lighthouse was purchased from Bartola Pacetti. This land was part of the grant given to Antonio Pons. The ten acres cost the government $400. Building materials were ordered, and by June, shortly after the drowning death of General Babcock, work began on the foundation. Things were looking good until there were

This group of young adults is seen enjoying the view from atop the Ponce Inlet Lighthouse. This is the second lighthouse built at the inlet. The first collapsed into the ocean in 1836 before it could be used. Construction on this tower was completed in 1887; it is the third-tallest lighthouse in the nation. It was added to the National Register of Historic Places in 1972 and designated a National Historic Landmark in 1998. *Courtesy of the State Archives of Florida.*

no funds appropriated in the 1884 budget. In March 1885, $40,000 was appropriated so that construction could continue. In August 1886, a further appropriation of $50,000 was made. As more materials were ordered, the pace of work increased, and by October 1886, more than 470,000 bricks had been put in place and the tower stood at 151 feet high. In March 1887, another $20,000 was appropriated, and by late summer the tower was complete.

Over the next few months, the two-thousand-pound first-order Fresnel lens was taken to the top of the tower piece by piece and then reassembled. During this time, the three keepers' quarters were finished, the oil storage building was completed and other final touches were done.

So sure of completion was Stephen Rowan, vice admiral of the navy, that he issued Notice to Mariners No. 25, which stated:

> *Notice is hereby given that, on and after November 1, 1887, a fixed white light of the 1st order will be shown from the Light-House recently erected at Mosquito Inlet, east coast of Florida.*
>
> *The apparatus lights 225 degrees of the horizon, and the focal plane is 160 feet above mean low water.*
>
> *The light should be seen in clear weather, from the deck of a vessel 15 feet above the sea, 18 nautical miles.*
>
> *The structure is a tower built of red brick, surmounted by a black lantern.*

Prior to sunset on Tuesday, November 1, 1887, principal keeper William Rowlinski and his assistant, Hardy Bryan, climbed to the top of the tower, each carrying a three-gallon can of kerosene that would be used to light the lantern. The light needed constant attention, and the keepers divided the night into shifts in order to allow for sleep. The addition of a second assistant keeper in December allowed for further sharing of duties and responsibilities.

Over the next fifty-six years, the lighthouse was tended to by six different keepers. Changes in technology kept them on their toes and eventually put an end to the need for a keeper. In 1953, the light was completely automated, and by 1970 the Coast Guard had shuttered the lighthouse, leaving it to be damaged by vandals. In 1972, the Ponce Inlet Lighthouse Preservation Association was formed and was instrumental in having the property deeded to the town.

In 1982, through the work of dedicated volunteers, a new tower deck was built, and the light was again lit. In 1998, the lighthouse was designated a

The dark red Ponce Inlet Lighthouse, shown here, is the second lighthouse built at the inlet. The first was built on the south side of the inlet and never used before it fell into the sea. The second lighthouse was built on more stable ground located on the north side of the inlet. It was completed in 1887. The light was acquired by the Town of Ponce Inlet in 1972 and is operated by the Ponce De Leon Lighthouse Preservation Association, Inc. The tower is open to the public; it is 203 steps to the top. *Courtesy of the author.*

National Historic Landmark. The property, including outbuildings, is open for tours, and visitors may climb the spiraling 203 steps to the tower deck. Once there, the incredible views are sure to mesmerize. What goes up must come down, and the climb down can often seem more difficult than that going up.[68]

7
Memories

So long as the memory of certain beloved friends lives in my heart,
I shall say that life is good.
—Helen Keller

In a city with as long a history as New Smyrna Beach, there are always going to be those places that no longer exist. Some are, of course, truly iconic and important to the story of the city, and others are just personal favorites of locals. They are still important nonetheless, and here we shall examine several of these pieces of New Smyrna Beach history that are no longer with us physically but still reside in our memories.

Alba Court Inn

This once-grand hotel stood near the foot of the Connor Bridge, offering winter guests easy access to the beachside, the Hillsborough (later Indian) River, the downtown area and more.

The building was constructed during 1905 and 1906 and opened for business during the fall 1906 season. A northwest wing was added during the spring of 1907. The inn consisted of twenty-six guest rooms, which were designed around the large atrium lobby. Many of the guests at the inn were escaping the frigid northern winters, and keeping them warm when Florida cooled

The Alba Court Inn was one of the once-grand hotels located in New Smyrna Beach. It was originally constructed in 1905 and 1906. The inn weathered many changes in the travel industry before eventually falling to the wrecking ball in 2007. The property it was situated on still sits vacant. *Courtesy of the author.*

was important. Fireplaces and Franklin stoves were the original forms of heat, and as time passed, these were upgraded. Lighting was provided by carbide gaslights. This same technology was used for car lights and mining helmets.

A 1917 sales brochure bragged: "$3 and up. Special by the week. Automobile and porter meet all trains." The inn

> *has been especially designed for those who desire a quiet house with table service at moderate prices. The house and all its equipment is new, modern and convenient. It has wide verandas, a cheerful parlor and large dining room, light and well ventilated sleeping rooms with running water in all of them, most of which are located on second floor, where baths and toilets are also located. The house is lighted by gas and electricity, and heated by hot water. Since the close of last season a number of private baths have been added, a large open fireplace has been built in the main parlor, the rooms have all been newly papered, new plumbing installed and many other improvements have been made to add to the comfort and convenience of the guest.*

Times continued to change, though, for the industry, and with the interstate system came the rise of hotels and motels located at more convenient travel junctions. In addition, travelers' tastes changed. No longer did northerners ride the train south to their destinations and need service to their winter homes. Many were driving or flying. They were more mobile. The wealthy also continued to find other destinations at which to spend their winters.

As the clientele changed, the costs of running such a large building mounted, and over the years the upgrades and repairs bragged about in 1917 were no longer financially manageable for newer owners. The once-proud inn became a home for lower-income seniors in many cases. Rather than glamorous winter guests, there were year-round tenants.

By 2006, the property had been sold to former New Smyrna Beach mayor Jim Vandergrifft and his wife, Pamela, for approximately $550,000. Zoning changes were put into place allowing for a three-story, sixty-three-bed assisted living facility, and in 2007 the Alba Court Inn, which was in a bad state of disrepair, was razed. By early 2013, the project was still not off the ground, and the Vandergriffts asked for a change in plans by requesting that a fourth story be allowed. The Historic New Smyrna Beach Preservation Commission recommended this be declined because it would not fit in with the surrounding neighborhood, but the city commission passed the exception and provided the Vandergriffts with an extension until April 1, 2014, to acquire building permits. This extension would have allowed them to also qualify for over $100,000 in CRA funds to help finance construction. By the April 2014 deadline, the proper permits had not been acquired, and the proposed funding was set to be distributed elsewhere. As of this writing, the large lot on the corner of Washington and Hillman Streets still sits vacant.[69]

BETHUNE BEACH

Volusia County is known to be a beach lover's paradise. Miles of hard-packed sand are available for bathers and sun worshipers nearly every day of the year. Flashback to the years prior to integration and this was not the case for African Americans. In stepped Mary McLeod Bethune and several wealthy black investors.

By December 1945, with World War II still fresh in everybody's minds, Bethune and others met in Tampa and formally signed a charter forming the nucleus of the group that would purchase the land that would become Bethune-Volusia Beach.

Mary McLeod Bethune was a leading force in education for African Americans. Her legacy includes Bethune-Cookman University. She was the visionary and namesake behind the creation of Bethune-Volusia Beach, an attempt to grant free and unrestricted beach access to African Americans. This land is now home to some of the most expensive homes in the area. *Courtesy of the State Archives of Florida.*

This charter stated there were to be 500 shares of stock with a value of $50 each. The total number of shares purchased by charter members was 386. Bethune herself purchased 28 shares. Owner Dana Fuquay was to be paid $132,000 for the beachfront property to the south of New Smyrna Beach.

Purchasers of stock that day were ensuring that African Americans had free access to the beach but were also making a financial investment. Bethune used her influence to advertise the opportunity to purchase beachside property in "a playground controlled exclusively by our race." Lots sized fifty by one hundred feet were available for as low as $590, and buyers from across the country swarmed to purchase a piece of paradise. By 1951, it was reported that more than five hundred lots had been sold.

As word of the beach spread and more people wanted to visit, it was decided that a resort to accommodate them was needed. In 1951, construction began on the Welricha Motel. By mid-1952, the fourteen-room motel was open, with each room having modern amenities. The reviews were overwhelmingly positive, and plans were made to expand the resort.

While things looked successful on the surface, Bethune-Volusia Beach was operating in the red, and it was imperative to find new investors. With the death of the beach's namesake in 1955, storm clouds were forming. While the beach and land purchases were available to whites, the goal was for Bethune-Volusia Beach to be a haven for African Americans, where they would be free to enjoy the beach without harassment from other beachgoers and law enforcement. Despite the lofty goals, the majority of properties sat unimproved. While many bought lots, it often proved difficult to actually build. This lack of action was due to several reasons: lack of financing, nonresident owners who didn't want to travel to Florida to supervise construction and, in some cases, a lack of interest in building.

In 1959, infrastructure improvements were needed. As a way to improve the overall community, several lots were deeded to Volusia County with the agreement that amenities such as an auditorium, a pier and picnic areas would be built. Unfortunately, it took over two decades for the county to make good on its agreement.

While the county dragged its heels, the country was changing. Integration was not just a dream but also the law of the land. Discrimination in public accommodations was now against the law. African Americans could go to any public beach they wished. They no longer needed to make the long trek to the south end of New Smyrna Beach. For many black property owners, it was time to sell. Many were able to sell their lots to speculators and investors for several times their original purchase price. With property prices rising, many others were unable to afford the tax liability and were forced to sell or risk losing their land. Historian Ashley Robertson has estimated that by the year 2000, only 8 of the nearly 750 residents in the Bethune-Volusia Beach area were African American.

The name of the community has been shortened to Bethune Beach. While many might know who Bethune is, this little-known chapter of not just New Smyrna Beach but also Florida and African American history continues to fade further into memory.[70]

THE CASINO

When we think of the term "casino" today, we think of Atlantic City, Las Vegas, slot machines and the like. From the mid-1920s until a devastating storm in October 1947, "casino" had a different meaning in New Smyrna.

Today, Flagler Avenue is a crowded and narrow road that provides a straight shot to parking and a beach entrance. The parking lot at the southeast end of Flagler Avenue was once home to an L-shaped, two-story wooden building called the Casino. The building was home to apartments that faced the beach on the second floor. On the first floor, facing Flagler Avenue, was a dance floor and snack bar last operated by owners Genevieve and Tex Zimmerman. It was a popular teen hangout serving sodas, sandwiches

The Casino was a well-known hangout in New Smyrna Beach. This view, looking east, shows that the building was located almost directly on the beach. While great for views, this proximity to the ocean ultimately led to the building being irreparably damaged during an October 1947 storm. This location now serves as a parking lot. *Courtesy of the author.*

Long a popular hangout for both youth and adult beachgoers, the Casino, which was located at the Flagler Avenue beach entrance ramp, met its end during a violent October 1947 storm that undermined the seawall and caused massive erosion. The building was severely damaged, and the property was eventually sold to the City of New Smyrna Beach. This photo shows the storm that would change the beachside appearance of the city. *Courtesy of the Southeast Volusia Historical Society.*

and alcoholic drinks to those of age. Mrs. Zimmerman said the Casino was a popular hangout for servicemen during World War II. Legend says that during Prohibition, it was common to find everybody, including the orchestra, with a flask of liquor.

During the first days of October 1947, a severe storm hit the area. Mrs. Zimmerman said it was something she would never forget. While authorities were quick to call it a "local disturbance" and not a hurricane or tropical storm, the strong storm surge and crashing waves caused massive damage to beachside homes and businesses. Despite the efforts of locals, including many high school students, the estimated eighteen thousand sandbags used were not enough to prevent large-scale erosion.

In the days following the storm, local police and the National Guard prevented unauthorized access to the beachside while authorities surveyed the damage. The erosion was particularly fierce at the Flagler Avenue beach entrance where the Casino was located. The storm surge undermined the seawall near the popular hangout, causing the wall to collapse and taking large amounts of sand with it. The structure was severely damaged, and when it was determined insurance did not cover this incident and banks would not step up to finance repairs, the remains of the building were taken down. The Zimmermans eventually sold the property to the city, and the area remains a popular one for beachgoers but for a different reason: parking.[71]

MOSQUITO LAGOON HOUSE OF REFUGE

Modern-day boaters have the luxury of the United States Coast Guard should they run into trouble in the Atlantic Ocean. With a motto of *Semper Paratus*, or "Always Ready," these brave men and women are ready when called on for search and rescue missions. While this is not their primary purpose, it is the one that is most often heard of.

The United States Coast Guard was formed in 1915, when the Revenue Cutter Service and the U.S. Life-Saving Service were combined. Today, there are over forty thousand men and women on active duty, along with a host of reserve and auxiliary members.

Today, New Smyrna Beach has a Coast Guard search and rescue station located at the north end near the inlet. In prior years, there was a station located at the south end of the island on land that is now part of Canaveral National Seashore. That station had begun service as a house of refuge.

The house of refuge program began in Florida in 1874, when the United States Congress ordered the U.S. Life-Saving Service to build five houses of refuge along the East Coast. These locations included Bethel Creek, Gilbert's Bar, Orange Grove, Fort Lauderdale and Biscayne Bay. By 1884, the federal government was again building and contracted with Mr. Francis M. Smith to construct five more houses. These were to be located at Smith's Creek, Mosquito Lagoon, Chester Shoals, Cape Malabar and the Indian River Inlet. Of these ten, the only one that is still standing is at Gilbert's Bar, in Stuart, Florida. It now serves as the House of Refuge Museum.

The building plans for these houses were all very similar. They were located close to the ocean and on the highest dune that could be found. This was to allow for the best views to the ocean and also to allow stranded boaters the best chance to find the houses and thus safety. Because of their proximity to the ocean and the constant threat of storm surge, high tides and just the general wear and tear of salt water, the homes were built of the highest-quality materials available. The builder used standard plans created by architect Francis Chandler. The houses measured fifty-four by twenty-five feet. They were two stories with four rooms: a bedroom, a kitchen, a dining room and a parlor. The upstairs was used as a loft and allowed anybody who was rescued a place to stay for a few nights.

It is believed that the Mosquito Lagoon house was home to five different keepers during its three decades of operation. Jacob Summerlin was the first keeper and served from June 1886 through August 1890. He was followed by Elwin Samuel Coutant, the longest-serving keeper. Coutant served from August 1890 until October 1912. The third keeper was F.W. Church, who served from October 1912 until January 1913. Church was followed by Frank Hayman, who was keeper from December 1912 until March 1913. The last official house of refuge keeper before the Coast Guard took over operation of the building was Lee Huntley, who served from February 1913 until the merger in 1915.

It took a special kind of person, and family, to be a house of refuge keeper. This was an isolated, lonely and sometimes dangerous life. The houses were oftentimes far from civilization, and the families had to be self-sufficient. It was required that keepers provide their own food supply and have enough on hand for anybody they rescued, whether it be from the ocean or a lost soul wandering the beach. Regulations stated that any party rescued would have to pay fifty cents per day for meals. This would prove to be nearly impossible to collect, however, and the government would usually end up reimbursing the keeper.

Being the child of a house of refuge keeper was not much fun. The constant isolation from others meant there was little opportunity to play with other children and make friends. School was often considered a luxury because of the distances that had to be traveled. Children at the Mosquito Lagoon House of Refuge could attend school in Oak Hill if they could be ferried across the lagoon. The chores were often difficult, as well. The building needed constant upkeep, rescue equipment needed to be kept in top working order, gardens needed tending and they could be called on to help with ocean or river rescues. This life did not suit Harold Coutant, the youngest son of Elwin, and at age twenty he ran away rather than risk being stuck. He finally settled in the Fort Pierce area.

After World War II, the house of refuge building was decommissioned by the Coast Guard and the property sold. The building then sat vacant and would be used by beach wanderers or those who were lost. Around 1950, the building was accidentally burned to the ground by a lost motorist who had taken shelter.

Today, there is really nothing to see of the building. It is possible to see where it was located and note why the location was chosen. The house was built at what is now Parking Area Number Five in the Canaveral National Seashore. During the construction phase of the parking lot and roads, archaeological surveys were completed that turned up ceramics, glassware and food remains. Visitors may learn more by visiting the Eldora State House, which is also on the Canaveral National Seashore property.[72]

OLD FORT PARK WATER TOWER

Almost every small town had one. They were impossible to miss since they stood head and shoulders above almost every building in town. New Smyrna Beach was no different in that the city had a water tower located in the downtown area. The New Smyrna Beach water tower was located in Old

The unusual concrete ring that sits in Old Fort Park has strong sentimental meaning to many longtime residents. This is the location where the water tower previously stood before being removed in 1994 due to its deteriorating condition. The water tower is most remembered for having been brightly decorated every Christmas season. *Courtesy of the author.*

Fort Park, and while it is no longer there, a lasting reminder of the tower remains in the form of a concrete outline of a circle located in the well-manicured grounds of the park.

The purpose of a water tower is to hold a supply of potable water at an elevation sufficient to provide enough pressure to allow for distribution of water in the event of a power outage. Once the supply of water in the tank is exhausted, however, it requires electricity to run the pumps in order to refill the tower. In addition, some towers were used to hold water for use by local fire departments should it be needed.

There was nothing really special about the water tower in New Smyrna Beach. It wasn't an unusual shape, it wasn't painted an unusual color and it didn't have a fancy logo of any kind on it. Rather, it was what the city did to the tower every Christmas that has brought the tower eternal fame. Each year, starting in 1953, workers from the local Utilities Commission hung strings of lights off the tower, creating a large "Christmas tree." These lights caused a dramatic reflection in the marina, and it has been said the lights could be seen for miles out at sea. For children, when they saw the lights, they knew it was getting close to the time for Santa Claus, and many families made it an annual tradition to see the lights.

The man behind the idea for adding lights to the tower was Wayne Lowe, a lineman at the time before being promoted through the years to the job of manager at the Utilities Commission's Transmission and Distribution Department. Mr. Lowe was known to put on a Scrooge persona when discussing the history of the lighted tower. It never lasted for long, however: "I don't know what got into me back then. I wish nobody would've listened. I sure thought it would look good, though."

From a small start of eight streamers of lights, the display grew until there were eighteen streamers. In 1957, a large lighted star was added to top off the tower and make the display truly unique. In total, the eighteen streamers and the star contained almost 1,300 bulbs. Each year on Thanksgiving night, the lights were lit to the joy of both young and old. They were kept off until the day of the Christmas parade—usually the first or second Saturday of December. They would then be lit each evening until New Year's Day.

The novelty of the lighted water tower led to many comments and good publicity for the city, some of it national in nature. During the inaugural year of the lights, visitors from Miami were quoted as saying that the lighting was as good as they had seen in any city. In 1956, former city manager John C. Ferris penned an article for the trade publication the *American City* titled "Water Tower Turns Christmas Tree." While mostly a boosterism piece,

The water tower that used to stand in Old Fort Park was decorated every Christmas season with dozens of lights. This view, looking west from the marina, shows just how brightly lit the tower was and why, to this day, it is still a popular Christmas memory for those who remember seeing it. *Courtesy of the author.*

it showcased for other city managers what New Smyrna Beach had created. In the December 1969 issue of *Southern Living*, the New Smyrna Beach water tower received national attention. A brief piece outlined the story of the water tower for the whole country to enjoy.

While it would seem that the job of hanging lights from the water tower would be a dangerous one that nobody would want to do, the opposite was true. It was considered a badge of honor to hang the lights, and annually Utilities Commission employees would put their names in a hat in hopes of being one of the chosen few to climb the tower. For some men, it was the allure of the extra pay, but for many it was for the joy it brought to the faces of residents.

After the treacherous climb up a nearly vertical ladder inside the tower, workers strapped on their safety belts and stepped outside. Walter Davis described the feeling in a December 1987 article in the *Orlando Sentinel*: "If the wind is blowing, you can feel the tower move and you have to keep one knee bent and the other straight to balance yourself." In 1985, Davis was quoted as saying, "On a clear day the view is unbelievable. You can see the VAB building at Cape Kennedy to the south, Ponce Inlet and Daytona Beach to the north and westward past Samsula." Despite the potential danger, no injuries were reported during the light hanging or removal.

Time, however, was rapidly catching up with the water tower, and the elements finally took their toll. In 1994, the once-proud tower was taken down as a safety precaution. Visitors to Old Fort Park can still find a trace of the tower, though. There is a concrete ring still left where the tower used to stand.

As for the Christmas decorations, all is not lost either. While there is no longer a giant Christmas tree that can be seen from miles out on the Atlantic, there is still an annual lighting event, and it features a large star similar to the one that used to stand on the tower. In 2011, Stuart Hughes began making preparations to bring back the old star for the "Light Up Canal Street" event. Unfortunately, the original star was in too poor a condition to be placed on top of the Utilities Commission building. With the help of local "fabricating wizards," a new, much lighter and more energy-efficient star was created. Now, future generations can feel the same joy their parents felt at the annual holiday lighting.[73]

The job of decorating the water tower each November was one that Utilities Commission workers were honored to have. The job was so prestigious that names were drawn out of a hat to see who would climb the tower in order to bring Christmas cheer to the town. It has been said that workers on top of the tower could see all the way to Cape Canaveral on a clear day. Here, workers are shown putting the finishing touches on a holiday display. *Courtesy of the author.*

Other Assorted Memories

New Smyrna Beach has more than its share of local legends—buildings and businesses that are no longer there but are firmly planted in the minds of longtime residents. To list them all would be a futile effort and one that would no doubt leave some readers flabbergasted that their favorite isn't listed. A special few deserve a brief mention, however.

Stella's Skyline Restaurant was a popular eatery located on the outskirts of New Smyrna Beach near the airport. For many years, it was the go-to place for birthdays, anniversaries and other milestone occasions. Here, one of the chefs displays a delicious dish. After Stella's closed, the building was home to several restaurants, but none has had the success and positive feedback of Stella's. *Courtesy of the Southeast Volusia Historical Society.*

Stella's Skyline and Leon's Restaurant were favorite restaurants for many locals and visitors. Stella's was located on U.S. 1 near the New Smyrna Beach airport. According to what I have been told, the food was always good, and this could be considered New Smyrna's first upscale restaurant.

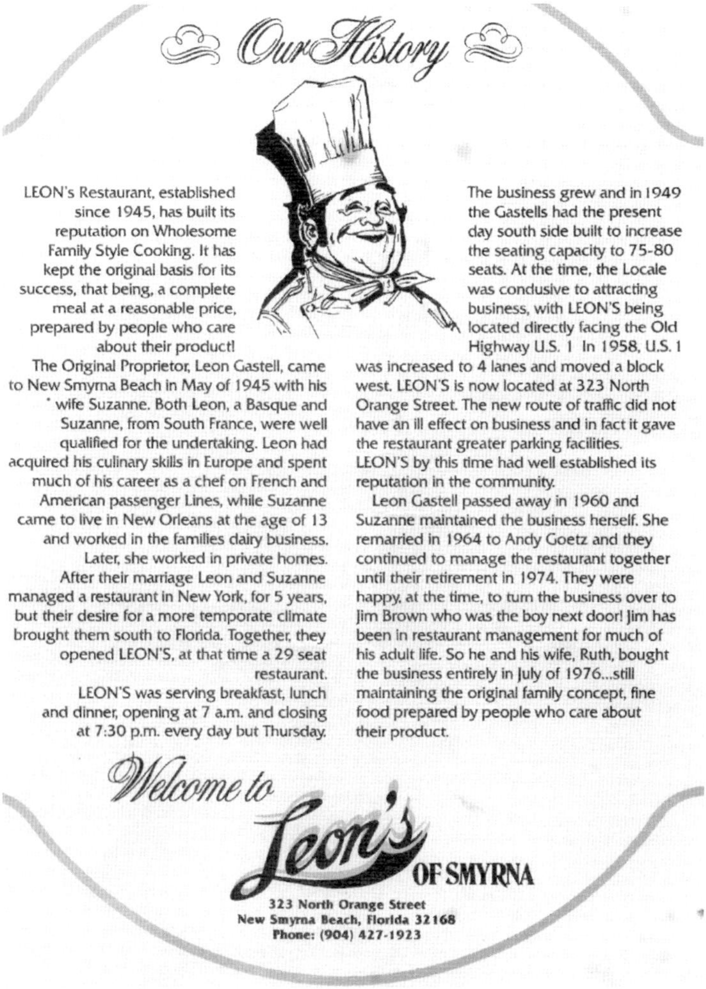

Our History

LEON's Restaurant, established since 1945, has built its reputation on Wholesome Family Style Cooking. It has kept the original basis for its success, that being, a complete meal at a reasonable price, prepared by people who care about their product!

The Original Proprietor, Leon Gastell, came to New Smyrna Beach in May of 1945 with his wife Suzanne. Both Leon, a Basque and Suzanne, from South France, were well qualified for the undertaking. Leon had acquired his culinary skills in Europe and spent much of his career as a chef on French and American passenger Lines, while Suzanne came to live in New Orleans at the age of 13 and worked in the families dairy business. Later, she worked in private homes.

After their marriage Leon and Suzanne managed a restaurant in New York, for 5 years, but their desire for a more temporate climate brought them south to Florida. Together, they opened LEON'S, at that time a 29 seat restaurant.

LEON'S was serving breakfast, lunch and dinner, opening at 7 a.m. and closing at 7:30 p.m. every day but Thursday.

The business grew and in 1949 the Gastells had the present day south side built to increase the seating capacity to 75-80 seats. At the time, the Locale was condusive to attracting business, with LEON'S being located directly facing the Old Highway U.S. 1 In 1958, U.S. 1 was increased to 4 lanes and moved a block west. LEON'S is now located at 323 North Orange Street. The new route of traffic did not have an ill effect on business and in fact it gave the restaurant greater parking facilities. LEON'S by this time had well established its reputation in the community.

Leon Gastell passed away in 1960 and Suzanne maintained the business herself. She remarried in 1964 to Andy Goetz and they continued to manage the restaurant together until their retirement in 1974. They were happy, at the time, to turn the business over to Jim Brown who was the boy next door! Jim has been in restaurant management for much of his adult life. So he and his wife, Ruth, bought the business entirely in July of 1976...still maintaining the original family concept, fine food prepared by people who care about their product.

Welcome to Leon's OF SMYRNA

323 North Orange Street
New Smyrna Beach, Florida 32168
Phone: (904) 427-1923

Always a local favorite, Leon's Restaurant was located on North Orange Avenue and was in business from 1945 until approximately 1996. When it opened, the business was situated on busy U.S. 1, but that changed when the highway was moved and widened in 1958. While Leon passed away in 1960, his wife continued to own the business until 1976, when it was sold to Jim and Ruth Brown. *Courtesy of the Southeast Volusia Historical Society.*

Unfortunately, one of the unique qualities about the restaurant—being located away from town at the airport—also was a problem when more conveniently located restaurants opened. In recent years, the building has held numerous other restaurants and now houses Lost Lagoon Wings and Grill. Leon's, which opened in 1945, was more centrally located at 323

North Orange Avenue. Prior to 1958, Orange Avenue was a part of U.S. 1. Even after the road move, Leon's was a popular restaurant, and the Gastell family served family meals at family prices until Leon passed away in 1960. Leon's stayed in the family until 1976. Leon's Restaurant closed in 1996.

Along with the Alba Court Inn, another of the grand hotels that used to serve New Smyrna Beach was the Hotel New Smyrna. This imposing building also went by the names Hotel Gordon, the Rio Vista Hotel, the Indian River Inn and the Indian River Lodge throughout the years. Originally built around 1916, it was open only for the winter season and catered to a wealthy clientele. Changes in travel styles, new ownership and the need for a more steady revenue stream led to changes for the hotel. Unfortunately, as often happens with large buildings such as this one, time, a lack of money and deterioration caught up with it, and the structure was demolished in 2005 after nobody came forward with funds to make the needed repairs and a business plan to keep it afloat.

It is said that many youngsters had their first jobs, and first kisses, at the Victoria Theater. The Victoria was conveniently located on Canal Street showing first-run films during what many call the golden age of cinema. Contemporary newspaper advertisements show short-run engagements of films with the day's biggest stars. During World War II, the theater was active in the war bond movement. The theater, which held just over five

The grand Hotel New Smyrna offered luxury accommodations to travelers starting in 1916, when it was named the Rio Vista Hotel. During "the season," this was one of the places to see and be seen in New Smyrna. The hotel went through several name changes over the years and was demolished in 2005 despite much public opposition. *Courtesy of the author.*

Time, the elements and a lack of money led to the demolition of the once-grand hotel that was known by several names over the years. These names included the Hotel New Smyrna, Hotel Gordon, Indian River Lodge, Indian River Inn and the Rio Vista Hotel. The hotel was demolished in 2005 after many efforts to save it. *Courtesy of the Southeast Volusia Historical Society.*

hundred people, ceased operating at its most famous location in November 1965, when Little Drug Co. expanded and took over the building. Despite having gone through several owners through the years, Little Drug is still considered the "hometown" pharmacy. It has an old-style lunch counter that is full every day. Some of the original theater fixtures are still in place, though they are not available for public viewing. The Victoria name still stands proud atop the building as a reminder to longtime residents of first jobs and first kisses.

Other gone but not forgotten locations include Feger's Fish Market, the Burger Chef at the corner of U.S. 1 and Highway 44, the Ocean House on Riverside Drive at the courthouse annex, Faulkner Avenue School, the old high school building on the north causeway, the Bank of New Smyrna, the Gulf Oil Plant, the Ice Plant, Davis Corner Store, playing shuffleboard on the mainland and more. These types of memories continue to be made each year as time moves on and businesses close or owners retire. A prime

This mid-1950s view is of the lawn bowling courts located at the corner of Sams Avenue and Julia Street. The Mainland Shuffleboard Club called these courts home for many years. The shadow that is seen on the courts is from what was then the post office. Note the building that housed city hall and the public library in the background. *Courtesy of the author.*

example that will be talked about for years is the fire station on Faulkner Avenue that is being rehabbed for future use but for many residents will always be the fire station.

APPENDIX A

Presidents of the Southeast Volusia Historical Society

Marvin Age	1982
Larry Sweett	1983–1984
Ray Goodrich	1985–1986
George Wolsfelt	1987–1988
Norman Orel	1989–1990
Peggy E. Wolfsfelt	1991–1992
Joanne Sikes	1993
Larry Sweett	1994–1995
Dolores Maylone	1996
Bobby Mattox	1997
Eugene Sheldon	1998–1999
Jim McGee	2000–2002
Dave Borland	2002–2005
Irene Beckham	2005–2007
Larry Sweett	2007
Rick Newell	2008–2011
John Peel	2011–2013
Larry Skates	2013–2015
Greg Holbrook	2015–

APPENDIX B

Mayors of New Smyrna and New Smyrna Beach*

P.L. Gaddis	May 1920–May 1924
William C. Chowning	May 1924–May 1928
William Edward Swoope Sr.	May 1928–June 1943
Frank F. Lee	June 1943–October 1943
Edward E. Altman	October 1943–April 1945
Julius "Jack" A. Sapp	April 1945–April 1946
Hugh K. Pierson	April 1946–April 1948
Dorcie E. Huffaker	April 1948–April 1949
Harrison M. Benham	April 1949–April 1950
Edward E. Altman	April 1950–April 1951
Dr. Carroll Byrd Jones	April 1951–April 1952
Bruce B. Sweat	April 1952–April 1953
Dr. Carroll Byrd Jones	April 1953–April 1954
Hannah D. Bonnet	April 1954–April 1955
Edward E. Altman	April 1955–April 1956
Breece A. McCray	April 1956–April 1957
Strobel J. Boll	April 1957–April 1958
Robert L. Arnau	April 1958–April 1960
Hannah D. Bonnet	April 1960–April 1962
William S. Hathaway	April 1962–April 1966
Robert C. Pattillo	April 1966–April 1970
Frederick Doster	April 1970–April 1972
Lowell A. Hanks	April 1972–March 1976

John R. Pletincks	March 1976–November 1977
George E. Musson	November 1977–April 1995
William D. Rogers	April 1995–August 1995
James L. Vandergrifft	August 1995–November 2007
Sally E. MacKay	November 2007–November 2009
Adam R. Barringer	November 2009–November 2014
James W. Hathaway**	November 2014–

*This list has been compiled with the help of Dave Miner and Barbara Zafuto at the New Smyrna Museum of History, along with Johnny Bledsoe, city clerk for the City of New Smyrna Beach.
**James W. Hathaway is the son of former mayor William S. Hathaway.

Appendix C

Mayor George Musson's Speech Dedicating the Lydia Pettis Memorial Plaque

This brief speech was given by New Smyrna Beach mayor George Musson on June 25, 1982, during a dedication ceremony for a monument and plaque in honor of Lydia Pettis that is located in front of city hall.

I would like to thank all of the dignitaries and many friends of Lydia Pettis for coming today to pay tribute to a fine lady that has done so much for this community of New Smyrna Beach and Southeast Volusia County.

Those of us gathered here today knew Mrs. Pettis for her dedicated community service and particularly for her kind and thoughtful concern for others. She was not only a pillar of good for the community but was also very dedicated to working for her church and the influence that the Christian religion has on all of us.

As we all know, Mrs. Pettis was founder of the Forgotten Christmas Tree Program, which provided a little Christmas cheer to many of the underprivileged people of our community every year during the Christmas holiday season. Although she had many helpers in this endeavor, it was Mrs. Pettis that always kept the enthusiasm for this idea progressing.

There is no question that Mrs. Pettis was a leader in all phases of community life. Many times, the city leaders would turn to Mrs. Pettis for her help and counsel when community problems would arrive. Her philosophy that everyone is created and should be treated equal was always important in easing any racial tensions that developed while she lived in New Smyrna Beach.

Many of you here today had close working relationships with Mrs. Pettis and her many community endeavors. I would like to recognize a few that worked closely with her and also helped further the idea of this plaque in her memory: Mrs. Mary Guiler, Mrs. Nickie Whol, Mrs. Ruth Johnson, Mrs. Celia Watson, my fellow city commissioners and staff of the city, just to mention a few, as well as all of you here assembled have had a part in working toward this fine memorial to Mrs. Pettis.

I'm sure we are very proud to dedicate this plaque to the memory of Mrs. Pettis, and we will have it as a permanent fixture in front of city hall to remind all of us of her graciousness and love of her fellow citizens.

Appendix D

Poem Commemorating the Coronado Beach Water Tower

To a Towering Friend

*Written by Margaret S. Pratt**

The tower stood there many years
Like a sentinel on high,
And it supplied the water
From its perch up in the sky.
It was a welcome landmark
It served to show the way
To many on the beach-side
Who had a tendency to stray.
To some it was a challenge
To climb up and look around.
To others something to look up at
With their feet firmly on the ground.
It hasn't supplied water now
For three or four years,
And the rusting of the nuts and bolts
Was beginning to cause fears.
So in they called a trusty crew
To take the big tank down.

Folks came to watch them
From all over town.
First with blow-torches flaring
Flames so very hot,
They cut in pie shaped pieces
The roof from off the top.
The main tank, they cut in two,
The bottom was in four,
Except for small connecting pieces
To keep them all secure.
They brought a great big crane
With boom so very high,
And one by one picked those pieces
From their perch up in the sky.
Many years from your stately height
You could see far and wide,
But like the waves upon the shore,
You've now reached your ebb-tide.
So now Good-bye Old Friend,
Your job has been well done.
We will find that you are missed
By many more than one.

*This unpublished poem was found in the archives of the Southeast Volusia Historical Society.

Appendix E

Names of Observers on the Watch and Warn AWS Monument*

J.L. Abernathy	Annis Ahl	Don Allen
Mrs. F. Allen	Ted Anderson	W. Ashmead
Lot Atkinson	Mrs. L. Atkinson	F.O. Bankston
Marina Bankston	L.S. Beaumont	J.M. Benton
Clive Bonnet	Hannah Bonnet	Jeanie Bonnet
Jewel Bouchelle	E.E. Bowden	R. Bowers
Mrs. R. Bowers	J.H. Bowman	Jim Brown
J.R. Bush	H.O. Buttery (?)	Mrs. H.R. Cabrara
Bert Calhoun	L.S. Carr	Mrs. M.M. Casilberry
M. Christian	Bert Colborn	Hilda Collins
Ruth Collins	Mrs. W.S. Collins	Chas. Davis
Mrs. J.C. Deal	F.M. Dulin	J.A. Eason
Mrs. I. Edgar	Barbara Elderton	Glenn D. Evy
Mrs. J. Falrant (?)	(?) Falrant (?)	Vernon Falrant (?)
W.J. Forster	Mrs. W.J. Foster	Don Galligher
J.A. Goodwin	K.C. Goodwin	Joan Guest
V.R. Hardy	F.A. Harris	Mrs. F.A. Harris
Joe Harris	John Harris	L. Hedges
F.H. Herring	Mrs. F.H. Herring	Jeanette Hinson
Mrs. H.C. Hinson	Norma Hotard	Pamela Hotard
E.W. Husky	Sol Inglas	Carol Johnson

E.M. Jones
Kit Kissam (?)
Frank Knight
Daisy Kreis
R.C. Kreis
Mary J. Lewis
W.C. McDuffie
M.J. McIver
Mrs. M.J. McIver
Francis McIver
Walter McKiver
J.L. McLaren
Don Miller
F.L. Moore
Pearl Moore
Wm. Moorehouse
Mrs. Wm. Moorehouse
F.S. Morris
Mrs. F.S. Morris
R.L. Mudrett (?)
A. Murphy
K. Muellel
V. Newell
Ann Nick
Glyn Owens
Mrs. M. Owens
Nial Pace
O.M. Poole
Petie Power
Martha Prine
Trius Robertson (?)
Virginia Rolfe
Mrs. J.G. Schauwecker
R.B. Schnee
Mrs. R.B. Schnee
Anna Shea
Edward Shea
Oliver Shirk
Rev. E.C. Simkins
Don Smith
M.A. Smith
E.B. Spurr
Mrs. E.B. Spurr
J.G. Stevens
Katherine Swoope
W. Tanner
Fred Tryon
Marlon Tryon
Mrs. Lena Vrooman
Mrs. R.R. Vrooman
C.L. Waidan (?)
Mrs. Geo Wallace
Henry Waters
Mrs. F.B. Watham (?)
J.C. Weager
D.C. White
Mrs. D.C. White
D.C. White Jr.
E.J. Wilcox
Mrs. E.J. Wilcox
Martha Wilcox
Ed Wilson
J. Reg Wilson
W.E. Wood
Mrs. W.E. Wood
W.G. Woodward
Mrs. W.G. Woodward

*This list has been taken from the May 29, 1999 *Rediscovered History* pamphlet from the Men's Garden Club of Volusia County.

APPENDIX F

Lighthouse Keepers at the Ponce Inlet Lighthouse*

PRINCIPAL KEEPER

William R. Rowlinski	October 13, 1887–November 30, 1893
Thomas P. O'Hagan	December 1, 1893–September 23, 1905
John Lindquist	October 3, 1905–June 30, 1924
Charles L. Sisson	July 1, 1924–August 16, 1926
James B. Butler	August 20, 1926–July 2, 1937
Edward L. Meyer	August 12, 1937–December 16, 1943

FIRST ASSISTANT KEEPER

Hardy Bryan
Lucius G. Stringfellow
Lewis S. Jervey Jr.
Charles N. Swan
Henry W. Bond
William T. Lindquist
Joseph Davis
Cardell D. Daniels
Walter Crook
Ludwell C. Damaree
James H. Carlin
Edna O. Elliot
Theodore S. Johansen
George B. Nauman
Rinaud Heisser
John R. Turner
Douglas Roderick
Edward L. Floyd
Victor E. Thelning
Walter C. Rowell
Pinckney L Whitely
Edward L. Meyer

Appendix F

Second Assistant Keeper

William Agee
John Abbott
Charles N. Swan
Charles Johnson
William T. Lindquist
Julius J. Jeffords
T.T. Gailand
Arthur F. Hodges
George Wallace
James H. Carlin
James A. Pine Jr.
Edward J. Praetorius
Pinckney L. Whitely
John D. Vann
Joseph D. Cooper
David C. O'Hagan
Lusius G. Stringfellow
John J. Joyner
Halvor Svendsen Jr.
John H. Minges
William S. Spencer
Joseph Davis
Benjamin F. Stone

Resident Coast Guard Personnel

Charner Smith
John W. Hicks
Henry Jones
Jesse Frank Howard
Carl "Sandy" Sanders
Herbert F. Smith

*This list was developed by Thomas W. Taylor and was included in his book *The Beacon of Mosquito Inlet: A History of the Ponce de Leon Inlet Lighthouse.*

Notes

Chapter 1

1. Library of Congress, Jeanette Thurber Connor Collection; *Tampa Tribune*, June 19, 1927.
2. Charles Henry Coe; Coe, *Red Patriots*, v.
3. Coe, *Debunking*.
4. Luther, *History of New Smyrna*, 72–77; *New York Herald*, March 4, 1894.
5. Fitzgerald, *Volusia County*, 141–43; Gold, *History of Volusia County*, 14–18.
6. Luther, *History of New Smyrna*, 74.
7. Fitzgerald, *Volusia County*, 181–83; Luther, *History of New Smyrna*, 72–77.
8. John B. Stetson Jr. obituary; *New York Times*, June 11, 1927; *Tampa Tribune*, June 19, 1927.
9. Coe, *Debunking*, 5–9.
10. Ibid., 9–13.
11. Ibid., 13–15.
12. Ibid., 15–24.
13. Ibid., 4, 28–29.
14. Redd, *Smyrna Life*, July 2014.
15. *Musqueto News* (April/May 2012).

Chapter 2

16. *Daily Journal*, January 15, 2000; *Daytona Beach News Journal*, March 19, 1974.
17. *Historic Edgewater New Smyrna Cemetery*.
18. St. Johns Rangers Sons of Confederate Veterans.

19. Hartman, *Biographical Rosters*, 1,614, 1,625.
20. *Daily Journal*, February 5, 2000; *Orlando Sentinel*, December 8, 1998.

CHAPTER 3

21. Gold, *History of Volusia County*, 125, 140–42.
22. Luther, *History of New Smyrna*, 106–08.
23. Interview with Barbara Zafuto.
24. Beckham, *History of SEVHS and Museum*.
25. National Archives and Records Administration, Washington, D.C., Applications for Headstones; *News Journal*, May 27, 1991.
26. Emory Bennett Medal of Honor citation. A copy is available in the Bennett file at the New Smyrna Museum of History.
27. *New Smyrna Beach Observer*, November 11, 1994.
28. Jane F. Smith letter, October 30, 1964, located in the Cultural Center file at the New Smyrna Museum of History; "Building of a Library in New Smyrna Beach, 1886–1976," located in the Libraries file at the New Smyrna Museum of History; *Daytona Beach Morning Journal*, March 17, 1941; *Downtown New Smyrna Beach Historic Walking Tour* brochure; *New Smyrna Beach Observer*, May 18, 1940; October 31, 1940; November 21, 1945.
29. Atlantic Center for the Arts; Florida Department of State Division of Cultural Affairs.
30. *Daytona Beach Morning Journal*, October 16, 1981; Hudson, *History of New Smyrna*, 21, 73; Lydia Pettis file, New Smyrna Museum of History. This file contains transcripts of newspaper articles about the Forgotten Christmas Tree program, a copy of her commendation from President Richard M. Nixon and more.
31. The Connor Library file located at the New Smyrna Museum of History contains a large number of newspaper articles regarding the controversy, saving, moving and subsequent restoration of the Connor Library. United Church of Christ New Smyrna Beach.
32. AHEPA; DAR.
33. *Daily Journal*, May 3, 1968; *Pelican*, April 25, 1968; May 2, 1968; May 9, 1968; undated and unnamed newspaper article, "Thanks Offered for Greek Settlers' Bravery 220 Years Ago."
34. Anonymous Chamber of Commerce History located in the Chamber of Commerce file at the New Smyrna Museum of History.
35. *Florida Catholic*, February 13, 1997; *News Journal*, November 22, 1997; *New Smyrna Beach Observer*, August 1, 1998; St. Rita's Colored Catholic Mission National Register of Historic Places Registration Form.

36. *News Journal*, August 15, 2014.
37. Ibid., February 6, 2005.

CHAPTER 4

38. Johnson, *History New Smyrna Lodge Number 149*; Leedham, *New Smyrna*, ch. 3.
39. Quoted in Griffin, *Old Fort Park*, 6.
40. Griffin, *Old Fort Park*, 17.
41. Ibid., 19–20.
42. Sheldon, "Seminole Attacks Near New Smyrna," 188.
43. Sheldon, *Stirring Incidents*, 2.
44. Ibid., 2–3.
45. *New Smyrna Daily News*, November 8, 1927; November 10, 1927; November 12, 1927.
46. *Pelican*, January 29, 1959.
47. *News and Observer*, November 7, 1982; November 12, 1982.
48. *New Smyrna Beach News*, November 1968.
49. *Daily Journal*, April 11, 1995.
50. Advertising brochure located in the AHEPA file, New Smyrna Museum of History.
51. *Observer*, October 16, 1998.
52. Gene Sheldon letter dated January 4, 1999, located in the AHEPA file, New Smyrna Museum of History; *Observer*, April 9, 1999.
53. *Daily Journal*, April 12, 2000; *Observer*, June 10, 1999; June 24, 1999; July 15, 1999.
54. Luther, *History of New Smyrna*, 78–81; Sweett, *New Smyrna, Florida.*

CHAPTER 5

55. Luther, *History of New Smyrna*, 115–19.
56. *New Smyrna Beach News*, July 2, 1937; July 31, 1937; August 2, 1937.
57. Luther, *History of New Smyrna*, 118–19; *New Smyrna Beach News*, May 2, 1945; May 17, 1945; March 21, 1946; March 28, 1946.
58. City of New Smyrna Beach Development Services LD-3-12: Charles Dummett Grave/Canova Drive, March 14, 2012; Redd, "Mysterious Single Grave Cemetery"; Strickland, "Dummett Family Saga."
59. *New Smyrna Beach News*, October 8, 1942; October 15, 1942; October 22, 1942. The Watch and Warn Monument file at the New Smyrna Museum of History contains items including undated newspaper clippings, an unpublished manuscript written by Harlan Hutchins titled "World War

II Watch & Warn Towers on the Southeast Coast of Volusia County, Florida" and a copy of the program from the 1999 rededication ceremony titled "Rediscovered History."

60. Parker, *Canaveral National Seashore*, 1.
61. *Eldora, Canaveral National Seashore.*
62. Moulton-Wells House National Register of Historic Places Registration Form; Parker, *Canaveral National Seashore*, 78–79, 91; *Smyrna Breeze*, August 10, 2004.

CHAPTER 6

63. Ponce Inlet.
64. Beckham, Ponce and Pacetti family information file; Fitzgerald, *Volusia County*, 176; Hartman, *Biographical Rosters*, 813; Taylor, *Beacon of Mosquito Inlet*, 11–16.
65. Taylor, *Beacon of Mosquito Inlet*, 5–7.
66. Ibid., 11.
67. "Design of the Mosquito Inlet Light Station," 4–8.
68. Ponce Inlet; Taylor, *Beacon of Mosquito Inlet*, 11–21.

CHAPTER 7

69. Alba Court file, New Smyrna Museum of History; *News Journal*, April 3, 2014; Volusia County Property Appraiser.
70. Cook-Wilson, *Isn't That God's Water*; Robertson, *Mary McLeod Bethune in Florida*, 67–78.
71. *Daytona Beach Morning Journal*, November 20, 1979; Luther, *History of New Smyrna*, 124; *New Smyrna Beach News*, October 3, 1947; October 10, 1947; Sweett, *New Smyrna, Florida*, 119.
72. Parker, *Canaveral National Seashore*, 50–53; Redd, "Mosquito Lagoon House of Refuge."
73. *Daily Journal*, July 7, 1994; *Hometown News*, November 25, 2011; *New Smyrna Beach News*, December 10, 1953; December 17, 1953; December 20, 1956; December 4, 1969; *Orlando Sentinel*, November 20, 1985; December 22, 1987.

Bibliography

Articles and Books

Central Brevard Mosquito Beaters. *The Way It Was 1997*. Memory Book. N.p., 1997.

Coe, Charles H. *Debunking the So-Called Spanish Mission Near New Smyrna Beach*. Washington, D.C., 1941.

———. *Red Patriots: The Story of the Seminoles*. Bicentennial Floridiana Facsimile Series. Gainesville: University Press of Florida, 1974.

Cook-Wilson, Ethel. *Isn't That God's Water? The Advent and Demise of Bethune-Volusia Beach Incorporated*. N.p., 2015.

Design of the Mosquito Inlet Light Station. Ponce de Leon Inlet Light House Station, April 2010.

Detwiler, John Y. *Early History of New Smyrna; First Settlement in America (Supplementary Addition [sic])*. N.p., n.d.

Fitzgerald, T.E. *Volusia County Past and Present*. Daytona Beach, FL: Observer Press, 1937.

Gold, Pleasant Daniel. *History of Volusia County Florida*. Deland, FL: E.O. Painter Printing Company, 1927.

Hartman, David, and David Coles. *Biographical Rosters of Florida's Confederate and Union Troops, 1861–1865*. 6 vols. Wilmington, NC: Broadfoot Publishing Company, 1995.

Hebel, Ianthe Bond, ed. *Centennial History of Volusia Co. Florida, 1854–1954*. Daytona Beach, FL: College Publishing Co., 1955.

Kress, L.M. *Yesterday's Treasures: A History Sketch of Florida's East Volusia County, What the Early Settlers of Volusia Found*. N.p., 1989.

Luther, Gary. *History of New Smyrna: East Florida with Illustrations*. 3rd ed., rev. New Smyrna Beach, FL: Luthers Publishing, 2009.

Parker, Susan. *Canaveral National Seashore Historic Resource Study*. Edited by Robert W. Blythe. Atlanta, GA: National Park Service, 2008.

Poertner, Bo. *Old Town by the Sea: A Pictorial History*. Virginia Beach, VA: Donning Company, 2002.

Redd, Robert. "Mosquito Lagoon House of Refuge." *Smyrna Life Quarterly* (Spring 2014).

———. "The Mysterious Single Grave Cemetery Located in the Middle of the Road on NSB Beachside." *Smyrna Life* (September/October 2014).

———. "Tall Tales of the Sugar Mill Ruins." *Smyrna Life* (July/August 2014).

Robertson, Ashley N. *Mary McLeod Bethune in Florida*. Charleston, SC: The History Press, 2015.

Sandler, Roberta. *A Brief Guide to Florida's Monuments and Memorials*. Gainesville: University Press of Florida, 2008.

Schene, Michael G. *Hopes, Dreams, & Promises: A History of Volusia County, Florida*. Daytona Beach, FL: News Journal Corporation, 1976.

Sheldon, Jane Murray. "Seminole Attacks Near New Smyrna, 1835–1856." *Florida Historical Quarterly* 8, no. 4 (April 1930): 188–96.

Southeastern Archaeological Research, Inc. *Archaeology of the New Smyrna Colony*. N.p., 1999.

Strickland, Alice. "The Dummett Family Saga." *Journal of the Halifax Historical Society* 2, no. 1 (n.d.): 3–13.

Sweett, Zelia Wilson. *New Smyrna, Florida in the Civil War*. N.p.: Volusia County Historical Commission, 1963.

Taylor, Thomas W. *The Beacon of Mosquito Inlet: A History of the Ponce De Leon Inlet Lighthouse*. N.p., 1993.

Internet Sources

AHEPA. http://ahepa.org/ahepa.

Ancestry. http://ancestry.com.

Atlantic Center for the Arts. http://www.atlanticcenterforthearts.org/dedication-sculpture-legendary-artist-doris-leeper.

Charles Henry Coe. http://emeraldmeinders.wix.com/capt-charles-h-coe?fb_ref=Default.

DAR. http://www.dar.org.

Florida Department of State Division of Cultural Affairs. http://dos.myflorida.com/cultural/programs/florida-artists-hall-of-fame/doris-leeper.

Florida Memory Project. www.floridamemory.com.

John B. Stetson Jr. obituary. http://www.americanantiquarian.org/proceedings/44817432.pdf.

Library of Congress. Jeanette Thurber Connor Collection of Floridiana Finding Aid. http://hdl.loc.gov/loc.mss/eadmss.ms011094.

New Smyrna Lodge 149 F&AM. http://newsmyrnalodge149.org.

Ponce Inlet. http://ponceinlet.org.

Saving Eighteenth-Century New Smyrnea: Public Archaeology in Action. http://www.presentpasts.info/articles/10.5334/pp.41.

St. Johns Rangers Sons of Confederate Veterans. http://www.florida-scv.org/Camp1360/confederate_veterans_buried_in_v.htm.

United Church of Christ New Smyrna Beach. http://uccnsb.com/index.php.

U.S. Gen Web. http://files.usgwarchives.net/fl/volusia/cemeteries/glencoe.txt.

Volusia County Property Appraiser. http://webserver.vcgov.org/Name_search.html.

MISCELLANEOUS SOURCES

Beckham, Irene. History of SEVHS and Museum. Unpublished typescript provided to the author.

———. Ponce and Pacetti family information file. Documents provided to the author.

City of New Smyrna Beach Development Services LD-3-12. Charles Dummett Grave/Canova Drive, March 14, 2012.

City of New Smyrna Beach, Florida. *Celebrating 50 Years of Progress, June 11–14, 1953*. 5th Annual Seaside Fiesta and Women's International Air Race Souvenir Program.

Downtown New Smyrna Beach Historic Walking Tour. Undated pamphlet.

Eldora, Canaveral National Seashore. Tri-fold pamphlet. National Park Service, n.d.

Griffin, John W., and Robert H. Steinbach. *Old Fort Park and Turnbull Canal System Archaeological Survey Project New Smyrna Beach, Florida*. St. Augustine, FL: Historic Property Associates, 1990.

Historic Edgewater New Smyrna Cemetery Take a Walk Into the Past. Tri-fold pamphlet, n.d.

Johnson, Thomas C. *History New Smyrna Lodge Number 149 Free and Accepted Masons of Florida Chartered Jan. 22, 1896: 100 Years of Freemasonry in New Smyrna Beach, Florida, 1896–1996*. N.p., n.d.

Leedham, Karen C. *New Smyrna Chapter #3, Order of the Eastern Star*. N.p., n.d.

Mary S. Harrell Black Heritage Museum

Cemeteries file

St. Rita Colored Mission file

Moulton-Wells House National Register of Historic Places Registration Form. United States Department of the Interior, National Park Service, 2001.
National Archives and Records Administration, Washington, D.C.
Applications for Headstones for U.S. Military Veterans, 1925–1941
National Archives Microfilm Publication: A1, 2110-C
Record Group Number: 92
Record Group Title: Records of the Office of the Quartermaster General
New Smyrna Museum of History Sheldon Research Library
AHEPA file
Alba Court file
Canals file
Casino file
Cemeteries file
Chamber of Commerce file
Churches file
City Hall file
Connor Library file
Cultural Center file
Emory Bennett file
Libraries file
Masonic Lodge file
Musqueto News (museum's printed newsletter)
Stone Wharf file
Veterans' Associations file
Washington and Jeanette Thurber Connor file
Watch and Warn Monument file
Sheldon, Rudolphus. "Stirring Incidents of the Civil War as It Related to New Smyrna, Told by the Late Rudolphus Sheldon." 3-page typescript. N.d.
St. Rita's Colored Catholic Mission National Register of Historic Places Registration Form. United States Department of the Interior, National Park Service, 2007.

NEWSPAPERS

Daily Journal
Daytona Beach Morning Journal
Florida Catholic
Hometown News
News-Journal
New Smyrna Beach Daily News
New Smyrna Beach News
New Smyrna Beach Observer
Orlando Sentinel
Pelican
Smyrna Breeze
Tampa Tribune

Index

About the Author

Robert Redd is a native Floridian with a longtime interest in history. He is a graduate of Stetson University with a degree in American studies. He is a member of the Florida Historical Society, Southeast Volusia Historical Society, St. Augustine Historical Society, the Civil War Trust and several other historical organizations. He currently serves as executive director of the New Smyrna Museum of History. This is Robert's second book. His first book, *St. Augustine and the Civil War*, was published by The History Press in 2014. Robert lives just south of the "World's Most Famous Beach" with his wife, Christina; dogs, Finley, Bessie and Jennie; and cat, Ignatius.